PORSCHE
Catalogs

A Visual History from 1948 to the Present Day

Turbo

PORSCHE
Catalogs

A Visual History from 1948 to the Present Day

MALLARD PRESS

An imprint of BDD Promotional
Book Company, Inc.,
666 Fifth Avenue,
New York, NY 10103

Mallard and its accompanying design and logo
are trademarks of BDD Promotional Book
Company, Inc.

First published in the United States of America in
1991 by the Mallard Press

ISBN 0-7924-5517-7

A QUINTET BOOK

This book was designed and produced by
Quintet Publishing Limited
6 Blundell Street
London N7 9BH

Creative Director: Terry Jeavons
Designer: Wayne Blades
Project Editor: Sarah Buckley
Editor: Laura Sandelson
Photographers: Ian Howes, Mirco Decet,
Trevor Wood

Typeset in Great Britain by
Central Southern Typesetters, Eastbourne
Manufactured in Hong Kong by
Chroma Graphics (Overseas) PTE Ltd, (Singapore)
Printed in Singapore by
Tien Wah Press (Pte) Ltd.

CONTENTS

INTRODUCTION

Porsche is one of those names which immediately conjures an image in the mind of fast cars and high-flying lifestyles. For over 40 years, the Porsche company has developed and produced unique sports cars which have transcended society barriers by possessing enough charisma for the rich and famous, while being produced in sufficient numbers to make them affordable by the less well-heeled enthusiast. All of the photographs and illustrations in this book have been taken from the many sales catalogues produced by the Porsche Company to promote its products over this period, and show not only the development of the vehicles, but also the changes in style and fashion which have taken place.

The influence of the name Porsche on motoring history stretches back for 50 years prior to production of the first car bearing the family name. Dr Ferdinand Porsche was born in 1875 in the Bohemian village of Maffersdorf. His father was a tinsmith with a small family business in the village.

After having worked with Jacob Lohner on the Lohner-Porsche electric car, Porsche was invited to join the Austrian branch of the German Daimler Company, which later became Austro-Daimler. He oversaw the development of the Prince Henry model, named after the 1910 Prince Henry Trials where works team cars took the first three places. This type of domination of motor sport events was to become a familiar feature of the cars associated with his name. In 1923, Porsche joined the parent Daimler Company in Stuttgart as Technical Director. He was responsible for designing an impressive line of cars which culminated in the 250bhp SSKL. He also wished to develop a smaller family car, but the board of Daimler-Benz considered this type of vehicle did not fit with the image they had acquired. So, in 1929 Porsche returned to his native Austria and to their largest car manufacturer, Steyr.

FAR RIGHT : *The four men responsible for the 356 are shown in this 1955 brochure page. They were Dr Ferdinand Porsche, designer of the Volkswagen, his son Ferry who revived the company after World War Two and set it on course to produce its own cars, Karl Rabe who engineered the first prototype, and Erwin Komenda who designed and styled the production car.*

When the Bodenkreditanstalt bank crashed in 1930, it took many companies with it, including Steyr. However, with some financial assistance from Adolf Rosenberger, a German racing enthusiast, Dr Ferdinand Porsche founded his own independent engineering design studio, setting up his offices in a small back street in Stuttgart, together with a team of 12 engineers, including his son Ferry, Karl Rabe and Erwin Komenda. These four men would, nearly twenty years later, be responsible for the design of the first Type 356 cars. However, in the intervening years the company known as 'Dr Ing hc Ferdinand Porsche GmbH' would be responsible for the design and development of motorsport machinery and road cars including the Volkswagen Beetle.

At the end of the war Dr Porsche was interned by the French for his involvement in these wartime projects. Despite being over 70 years old and in poor health, he survived nearly two years of imprisonment and was released in 1948 to rejoin his family in Stuttgart, where his son Ferry had re-established the family business and had built a prototype of what would be their first production sports car, the 356.

In 1939, Porsche had designed and built for VW three special aerodynamic coupes based on the VW chassis

It's our Hobby to Build Your Hobby

Prof. Dr. Ing. h. c. F. Porsche, *whose sobriquet was "the Wizard", the man under whose ingenious hand the most famous developments of the Automobile Age were created, from the wheel hub engine to the Auto Union's world record car, from the torsion rod spring to the VW. His creative life covered a span of 50 years; his store of knowledge was invaluable. Great and many were the honors bestowed upon him, but he always remained the quiet, modest man who lived only for his work and his great idea.*

In 1921 a Viennese automobile journal wrote "Young Porsche proved that he was a perfect driver". In that year **Ferry Porsche,** *the son of the founder of the Porsche KG., was 12 years old and already driving his own small sports car. Today he is carrying on the tradition of his inventive father. While Prof. Porsche was still alive, Ferry Porsche set up new milestones in automobile history by creating the Cisitalia racing car and developing model 356.*

The cradle of Chief Engineer **Karl Rabe** *stood in Lower Austria. He has been working with Porsche almost without interruption since 1913. The old professor employed Rabe as a stripling of 17 years because he had already developed the best and simplest solution of a difficult tractor problem. Although he has been solving weighty technical problems for over a generation, he is not a scholarly dreamer but has remained a typical amicable Austrian.*

"There is one thing wrong with these people" said an eminent journalist after interviewing **Erwin Komenda,** *"they are too modest". Komenda, chief of the body designing department has been with Porsche for over 20 years. He created the Volkswagen body and is responsible for the much admired form of model 356: a man who thinks technically but brings forth artistic creations. His work is progressive in the best sense of the word.*

As early as 1910 Porsche realized that it was possible to increase driving speed by reducing air resistance. The result was the "tulip form" of the Prinz Heinrich car

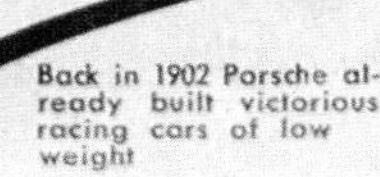

Back in 1902 Porsche already built victorious racing cars of low weight

and mechanics. These were intended to compete in the Berlin to Rome road race, but the outbreak of hostilities cancelled the event. After the war Ferry Porsche took this basic design and, with the assistance of Karl Rabe, turned it into a mid-engined two-seater roadster. After encouraging trials, Erwin Komenda designed a new body which transformed the prototype into a road-going two-seater coupe, with the rear-mounted engine layout which was to become so familiar. The early cars had flat-four cylinder 1100cc engines developing just 44bhp, but because of the low weight and streamlined shape, the cars were capable in excess of 80mph (128kph).

1953 saw the introduction of the now famous Porsche Crest. The basic design of this is attributed to Max Hoffman who, as the influential sole US importer of the marque, was responsible for a lot of the subtle marketing innovations at Porsche during the 1950s. Apparently during lunch with Ferry Porsche one day in New York, he said that he felt all car makers should have an emblem, and as Porsche did not, he quickly sketched an heraldic device onto a napkin and handed it to Porsche. The eventual design combined the coats-of-arms of the West German State of Baden-Wurttemberg and its capital city, Stuttgart, home of the Porsche works. However, rather than being emblazoned on the outside of the car, Porsche placed it in the centre of the steering wheel, perhaps signifying that the driver's pleasure is always their prime concern.

The 356 was evolved by continual development until in 1964 a new car emerged. This was called the 901 and featured a 6-cylinder 2-litre engine, but was rear-mounted and air-cooled as before. Quickly redesignated 911 to avoid clashes with Peugeot's model numbering system, this car was larger than the 356 and initially did

ABOVE: *This 1967 photo shows the Porsche logo which originated in 1953, derived from an idea sketched on the back of a New York restaurant napkin by Porsche's US importer, Max Hoffman.*

Who does all the thinking for PORSCHE?

The Porsche car is "merely made" at Stuttgart-Zuffenhausen, with the design and development functions being carried out a little way away in the countryside of Weissach.
Hardly anyone expects a so-called "small factory" to have such a large and lavishly equipped research centre.
A total area of approximately 450,000 sq. metres (4.8 million sq. ft).
About 1000 employees.
13,400 sq. metres (144,235 sq. ft) of workshops, test rooms and laboratories.
Two race tracks - one high speed Can-Am circuit, and one "mountain" circuit. Test tracks also for cross country, destruction and reliability tests - all of an inconceivable degree of severity.
A huge skid pad of 190 metres (624 ft) diameter. Other test and research facilities of our own design which others have still deemed too stringent for their products,
with rolling road dynamometers, special chambers where all types of weather conditions and driving effects can be studied so,
if comparison tests are required, the artificial test conditions can be reproduced exactly,
with all technological and scientific equipment for the in-depth research in the fields of overall driver safety, fuel consumption, pollution and accident damage minimisation.
Therefore, if the Porsche is better in styling, safer in general handling, more economical to run and more suitable for everyday use than other motorcars, you have to thank Weissach!

But all the research and development we do for our current and future models, racing cars, rally cars - for ourselves and our customers - only utilises our resources by about a third.
The other two-third's capacity is available to those who wish to avail themselves of our professionalism. So we design and develop anything for anyone who wants absolute safety of operation, precision or perfection - from heavy tracked vehicles to light weight motor-cycles - from the first thoughts on paper to the prototype, from the scale model to the first pre-production model.
So while we are very proud to tell you of the facilities and type of work we undertake, you will appreciate - we hope - that we cannot let you in to see for yourself on whose products we work!

LEFT, 1976: *Work commenced on the development of the Weissach Research Centre in 1961, and over 2,500 people are now employed there. The facilities include a full race circuit as well as the racing team's workshop.*

BELOW: *Another 1967 shot shows work taking place in the design centre. As well as carrying out its own design work, Porsche is a major sub-contractor, providing its expertise to many different fields of engineering.*

not receive the approval of the *cognicenti*. In 1975 a turbocharged 3-litre version was introduced. Although still using the same basic bodyshell, this had started to sprout spoilers and wheel arch extensions to cope with the added performance and increased wheel sizes needed. A further increase in capacity to 3.3 litres produced the awesome RS Turbo with a top speed of in excess of 160mph (267kph), and acceleration and handling to match. Further developments of the car have continued right up to the present day producing more power and refinement, as well as four-wheel drive and clutchless gear changes all of which should ensure that the 911 remains in production for many more years.

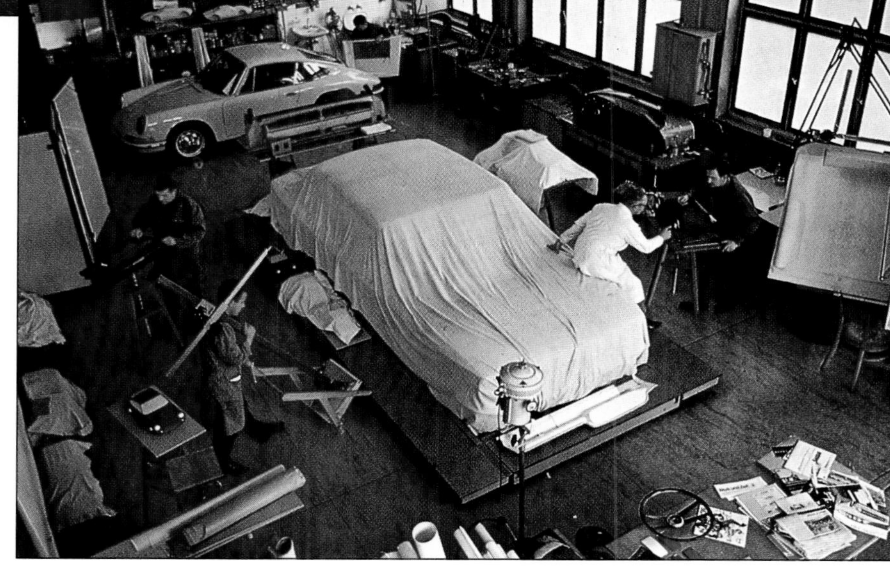

Manufacturing:

Swabian thoroughness.

Every Porsche is a unique creation. The carefully planned production sequence, strategically-positioned work stations, and critical system of checks and tests ensure that every Porsche comes off the line and to its new owner as a proud example of outstanding Swabian precision.

Pioneering achievements.

The 4-cylinder 924 and 924 Turbo are not merely a new standard for Porsche performance capability. They are expanding the horizons of automobile production as a whole with an impressive array of advanced technologies.

Porsche makes extensive use of hot-dip galvanized sheet steel for the bodies of all of its series, leading the way in the automotive industry. The manufacturing problems this process presented were monumental. The deep-drawing characteristics of the sheet metal and drawing tools had to be examined. Since zinc is softer than steel, suitable deep-drawing lubricants, preservatives, and transport pallets had to be developed to protect zinc surfaces of deep-drawn body parts from damage.

Yet another example is the difficulty inherent in obtaining color uniformity and adhesion on metal and plastics. New enamel systems were developed to resist cracking, splintering, and peeling, even under extreme deformation of elastic polyurethane body parts.

28

LEFT, 1978–82: *All the 924 production took place at the old NSU factory at Neckarsulm. The 944 was also produced there up until 1990, when plans were laid to centralise oil production at Zuffenhausen.*

The 911 SC Engine: A Compact Power Pack

The air-cooled 3-litre, rear mounted, engine is designed to stand up to continuous use.

The horizontally opposed engine has a bank of three cylinders on either side of the crankcase. This makes for compactness and low height so desirable in a sports car. The overhead valves are in an inverted V-pattern, and are operated by rockers and a single camshaft on each bank of cylinders. The forged crankshaft is meticulously balanced and rigidly located by eight main bearings. A dry sump lubrication system (found generally only in racing cars) ensures that even under high cornering stresses, the maximum amount of cooled and filtered oil is delivered to each lubrication point. A new tubular type oil cooler, with greater cooling capacity, keeps the oil temperature down in both the 911 SC and 911 Turbo even more efficiently.

The automatic start enrichment, incorporated in the fuel injection sytem, ensures immediate ignition and tick-over, even from cold. The Bosch K-Jetronic fuel metering system provides absolutely uniform filling of the combustion chambers for economy of use and clean exhaust emissions.

The contactless HT capacitor discharge ignition system does not need adjusting and is, therefore, service-free.

LEFT, 1978–82: *Despite the advances in automated production methods, a large proportion of the 911 is still assembled by hand.*

Yet exhilarating as the 911 is, by the mid-70s the Porsche engineers had realized that there was a better way of doing the same thing. This view was to evolve into the 928, but first came an interesting if somewhat accidental development. Porsche had been involved in designing a new sports coupe for Audi which would be conventional in layout with a front-mounted, water-cooled engine and rear-wheel drive. When this project was cancelled by Audi, Porsche considered it far enough developed to go ahead themselves and so it became the 924. This car fulfilled a long-standing requirement for providing a new, lower price-level entry point to Porsche ownership which had never been fulfilled by previous attempts with the 912 and 914 models. Once again, it was received with little initial enthusiasm by those chauvanistic enthusiasts who saw it as the beginning of the end for their beloved 911, nicknaming it the 'Hausfrau Porsche' because of the growing number of female owners it attracted. Although not universal, this short-sighted viewpoint overlooked the benefit of the large numbers of drivers who would be converted to Porsche ownership, and thus increase demand for the 'real' machines by their subsequent purchases. In 1982, the logical development of the 924 emerged in the shape of the 944. With a new engine and more muscular bodywork styling, the car was an instant hit and within 18 months of introduction accounted for just over half of all Porsche production. With subsequent increases in engine capacity and the introduction of 16-valve cylinder heads, the latest evolution, the 3-litre 944S2 has performance virtually equal to that of the latest 911 Carrera 2.

BELOW, 1964: *With each brave departure from the old formula, Porsche has risked the disapprobation of many 'Porschephiles'. In 1964 some fans of the 356 believed the 911 lacked its predecessor's character. Over two decades later 911 owners would feel the same way about the 944.*

The 924 cushioned the reaction to Porsche's planned departure from the rear-engined formula in the 928, which was also the first Porsche where the design had started from a clean sheet of paper, there being no carry-overs in components or previous development project influences. It had all of the performance characteristics of the 911 but without any of the histrionics. Gone were the bulbous wheelarches, whale-tail spoilers and strident exhaust note. What was left was a true 1980s *Gran Turismo* car, no frills, just clean, efficient aerodynamic lines, enough power and torque to outrun all but a few road cars and handling not only as good as the 911, but more reassuring. All of this was enough to win it the 1978 European Car of the Year Trophy, the first time that a specialist manufacturer had received this accolade. As with all other Porsches, the 928 has received continual development since its introduction, culminating with the 928S4 and GT models which now boast 5-litre engines, 4 cams and 32 valves, giving performance equivalent to the 911 Turbo.

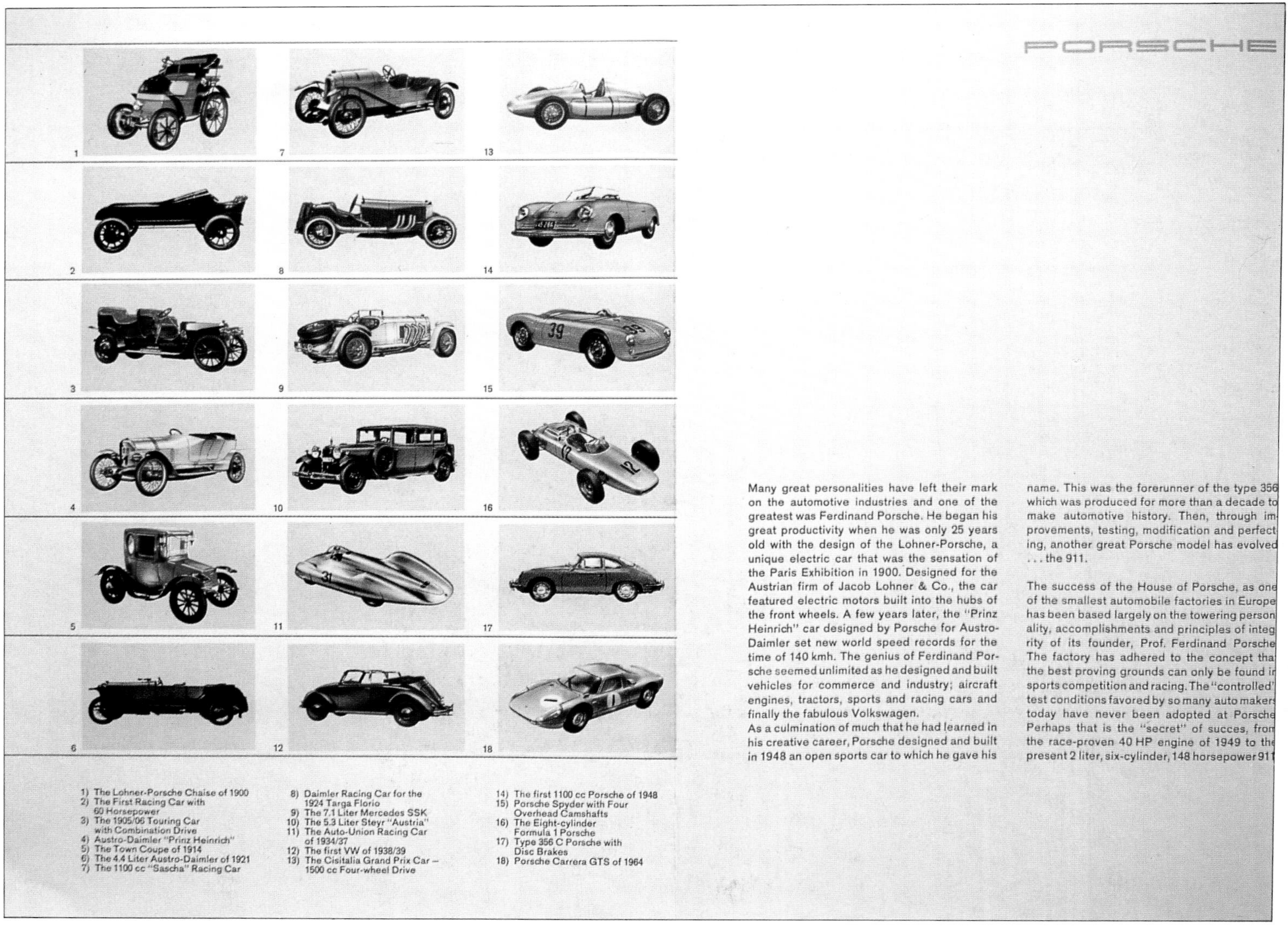

PORSCHE

1) The Lohner-Porsche Chaise of 1900
2) The First Racing Car with 60 Horsepower
3) The 1905/06 Touring Car with Combination Drive
4) Austro-Daimler "Prinz Heinrich"
5) The Town Coupe of 1914
6) The 4.4 Liter Austro-Daimler of 1921
7) The 1100 cc "Sascha" Racing Car
8) Daimler Racing Car for the 1924 Targa Florio
9) The 7.1 Liter Mercedes SSK
10) The 5.3 Liter Steyr "Austria"
11) The Auto-Union Racing Car of 1934/37
12) The first VW of 1938/39
13) The Cisitalia Grand Prix Car – 1500 cc Four-wheel Drive
14) The first 1100 cc Porsche of 1948
15) Porsche Spyder with Four Overhead Camshafts
16) The Eight-cylinder Formula 1 Porsche
17) Type 356 C Porsche with Disc Brakes
18) Porsche Carrera GTS of 1964

Many great personalities have left their mark on the automotive industries and one of the greatest was Ferdinand Porsche. He began his great productivity when he was only 25 years old with the design of the Lohner-Porsche, a unique electric car that was the sensation of the Paris Exhibition in 1900. Designed for the Austrian firm of Jacob Lohner & Co., the car featured electric motors built into the hubs of the front wheels. A few years later, the "Prinz Heinrich" car designed by Porsche for Austro-Daimler set new world speed records for the time of 140 kmh. The genius of Ferdinand Porsche seemed unlimited as he designed and built vehicles for commerce and industry; aircraft engines, tractors, sports and racing cars and finally the fabulous Volkswagen.

As a culmination of much that he had learned in his creative career, Porsche designed and built in 1948 an open sports car to which he gave his name. This was the forerunner of the type 356 which was produced for more than a decade to make automotive history. Then, through improvements, testing, modification and perfecting, another great Porsche model has evolved . . . the 911.

The success of the House of Porsche, as one of the smallest automobile factories in Europe has been based largely on the towering personality, accomplishments and principles of integrity of its founder, Prof. Ferdinand Porsche The factory has adhered to the concept that the best proving grounds can only be found in sports competition and racing. The "controlled" test conditions favored by so many auto makers today have never been adopted at Porsche Perhaps that is the "secret" of succes, from the race-proven 40 HP engine of 1949 to the present 2 liter, six-cylinder, 148 horsepower 911

ABOVE, 1964–66: *This page shows some of the cars which Porsche has designed, including many of the pre-war projects such as the Lohner, Wanderer and Volkswagen.*

But the ultimate road-going Porsche, at least for the moment, was yet to come. In 1981 at the Frankfurt Motor Show, Porsche showed a static design study based on the 911 which was intended to be developed into a Group B rally car. In 1984 that project made its debut in the Paris-Dakar rally, which it won. More successes followed and in 1986 Porsche announced a limited production run of 250 cars, some of which would be available for sale as road cars. Thus the 959 became the world's first 200mph (320kph) Supercar and once again pushed back the barriers of automotive design in a way that few other manufacturers can even contemplate.

RACING HISTORY

Porsche designs have always evolved because of the amount of competition work put in both by the works teams and private entrants. As early as 1910 Dr Porsche was winning motor sports events in convincing style. In the 1920s, the Mercedes SSK series had a distinguished competition record and in the early 1930s, he was commissioned by Auto Union to produce their Grand Prix machines. Together with Mercedes-Benz, the silver German cars were to dominate Grand Prix racing until the outbreak of war in 1939. The Auto Union's specification featured a mid-mounted engine developing some 600bhp driving the rear wheels with the gearbox mounted aft of the rear axle. The driver sat well forward of the fuel tank and the car had independent suspension via torsion bars. If this sounds familiar then it should, because these are some of the features of a modern Formula One car, but remember this was 1934 when the driver usually sat over the rear axle staring down a huge bonnet using the radiator cap to aim the car.

Needless to say the Auto Union required a different technique for driving, and not many drivers came to grips with it. The notable exception was Bernt Rosemeyer, an ex-motorcycle racer. Although the car had power and performance almost equivalent to current Formula One cars, it only had tyres which were 6 inches wide. Add to this fact that the road surfaces were indifferent, the tracks narrow, and there were no crash barriers or enforced safety regulations such as helmets, then you will realise that these were brave men indeed. That the cars were fast is indisputable. In their first German Grand Prix at Avus in 1934, a fast track outside Berlin recently returned to use, the Auto-Union set a new lap record of 140.33mph (227kph). Current F1 lap records on the faster tracks are not much different from this. In those days there were no driver's or manufacturer's championships, but if there had been Bernt Rosemeyer and the Auto-Union would have won them in 1936.

In the 1950s it was not unusual for a Porsche owner to collect his new car from the works in Weissach, and run it in by driving down through Switzerland and Italy to take part in an endurance road race such as the Targa Florio. After finishing, which he almost undoubtably would, he would drive back home across Europe. All of the development work on the racing 356 series cars was carried out in this fashion and resulted in the 4-cam Carrera 1600 engines and the works RSK Spyders. The

RIGHT, 1977: *Here a privately-entered RSR Carrera is being lapped by the works 936, in the first round of the European Championships in 1976. It was leading easily when a jammed throttle cable forced a long pit-stop, dropping it to third place. The black was considered unlucky, and the cars were repainted white.*

BELOW, 1989/90: *This brochure shows action from the highly popular 944 Turbo Cup series in Europe.*

SUCCESS IS THE BEST PROOF

The quality of Porsche engineering and technology has been proven under the arduous conditions of international motorsport. Nowhere else is the challenge greater or the results more immediate. Motor racing provides the ideal proving ground for the Porsche designers to develop advanced performance technology and test new engineering solutions.

With advances in performance, safety, durability and efficiency directly resulting from Porsche's commitment to motorsport, the benefits of this racing experience are there for every Porsche driver to enjoy.

The racing success of the 944 Series is absolute proof of the advantages of the Porsche Transaxle design, with a front mounted 4-cylinder engine balanced by a rear mounted gearbox.

The 944's motorsport career started with the toughest test possible. In 1981 Porsche entered a 944 Turbo, racing under the codename 924 GTP, at Le Mans and won the award for optimum reliability and least time spent servicing in the pits.

Soon after, a standard 944 Turbo road car, equipped even with a catalytic converter, won the challenging 24-hour race at Nelson Ledges in the USA.

Since this auspicious start, the 944 Series has been victorious on circuits throughout the world. Most recently, the 944 Turbo Cup Championship, again using production standard cars equipped with catalytic converters, allowed the car's full performance potential to be demonstrated under the most competitive conditions.

From the earliest days, a commitment to motorsport has been the foundation of Porsche's engineering and design philosophy. Whether at Le Mans, the Targa Florio, the Paris-Dakar Rally, Silverstone or the Nürburgring, Porsche technology has proven victorious time and time again. Today, the benefits of that commitment can be appreciated by every Porsche driver, nowhere more so than with the 944 Series.

1
MARTINI
PORSCHE

ABOVE, 1955/56: *From its early days, the 356 notched up regular racing successes. This provided good publicity for the launch of the Carrera models in 1955, by which time Porsche could boast a hat-trick of German Championships.*

- PORSCHE won the 1,100 c. c. class at Le Mans in 1951, 1952, 1954 and 1955 and the 1,500 c. c. class in 1953, 1954 and 1955. In 1955 a Porsche Spyder was over-all winner according to index.
- PORSCHE took first, second and third place in the 1,500 c. c. class at the 1955 Tourist Trophy.
- PORSCHE won the 1,100 and 1,500 c. c. production sports car classes of the Mille Miglia in 1952, the Gran Turismo classes up to 1,600 and 1,300 c. c. in 1953, 1954 and 1955; moreover the Spyder carried the 1,500 c. c. racing sports car class in 1954 and 1955.
- PORSCHE won the 1,500 c. c. class at the 12 Hours of Reims in 1954.
- PORSCHE won "its" class at Mexico's Carrera Panamericana in 1952, 1953 and 1954.
- PORSCHE won the production sports car class of the 1955 Grand Prix of Sweden, and at the Nürburgring, Europe's toughest race course, PORSCHE has carried top honours in the Gran Turismo and sports car classes every year since 1952.

LEFT, 1955/56: *Racing success has always been a powerful marketing tool for Porsche.*

RSK Spyders featured mid-mounted engines and evolved into the 904, to many eyes still the most stylish Porsche ever. Sadly the 904 did not last for long because with the introduction of the 911 and its new engine, this was quickly evolved into 6- and then 8-cylinder racing units which were used in the highly successful 908 series of cars.

Porsche was beginning to sweep all before it in the sports racing category, except at Le Mans where Ferrari and Ford had become the dominant teams. So, in great secrecy, Porsche designed its ultimate weapon, a 4.5-litre flat-12 air-cooled engine mounted in an all new bodyshell. This was the legendary 917 which won virtually every major race from 1970 until the rules of the formula were changed in 1974 and Porsche withdrew from this category as a works entrant. This was not the first time that Porsche had been so successful as to almost force the opposition to lobby for change. A few years earlier they had developed a Can-Am version of the 917 which simply ran away from the rest of the field, even though the opposition was mainly powered by giant 7- and 8-litre V-8 engines developing massive power outputs. It was also rumoured that a turbocharged version of the flat-12 engine had been run on the test bed and developed over 1000bhp, and this was in 1972!

Porsche returned to sports racing in 1982 with the 956 series and once again swept the board, winning the world championship and, along the line, finishing 1st, 2nd and 3rd at Le Mans on their first official outing for eight years. They dominated the category for the next five years, and even now the 962, a further development of the 956, is still highly competitive amongst much newer designs. Probably the most amazing statistic is Porsche's record at Le Mans, still the world's most gruelling motorsport test. From their first appearance in 1951 until 1965, a Porsche only once failed to take a class win. From 1965 to 1990, when this book was written, at least one Porsche has finished in the top five overall, including a total of 12 outright victories.

But one prize still remained. No Porsche project had been successful in Grand Prix racing since the demise of the Auto-Union in 1939. An attempt was made in the early 1960s to produce a Grand Prix car, but although it won some races, it was never really a serious contender for the championship honours. Then in 1983 McLaren Cars signed a contract with Porsche for the development of an all-new 1.5-litre turbocharged GP engine, with the aid of sponsorship from the Saudi Arabian engineering company, Techniques Avant Garde. So was born the TAG Turbo engine which powered the World Championship winning McLaren MP4 to victory in three consecutive seasons. After 45 years Porsche products were back at the top of one of the most glamorous sports in the world.

LEFT, 1976: *The Martini-racing Carrera Turbo RSR provided the basic research for the road-going Turbo variants which first appeared in 1975.*

356

The 356 was the first car put into series production by Porsche. It was an evolution from a project design for an aerodynamic coupe based on Volkswagen mechanical components which was produced just before the Second World War, but never raced as intended. Production started in 1948 when the car featured an 1100cc engine developing 40bhp and ended in 1965 with the Carrera 2 2-litre engine developing 130bhp. This demonstrated the Porsche philosophy of design evolution which features throughout their production history.

The production design was based around a pressed steel platform chassis with welded box-section sills and a central tunnel section to add stiffness as well as providing space for wiring and controls. The first 50 car bodies were hand-built, but after the move back to Stuttgart in 1950, body production was sub-contracted to Reutter Karosserie in order to increase the rate of deliveries in line with the demand from customers.

The engine was basically Volkswagen with Porsche modifications to the cylinder heads and carburation. This was sited at the rear and drove the car through a standard Volkswagen four-speed non-synchromesh gearbox. Suspension was fully independent, with parallel trailing arms at the front and swing-axles at the rear supported on flexible trailing arms.

Springing was provided by transverse torsion bars with telescopic dampers at the front and lever-arm type at the rear. Brakes were initially mechanically-operated drums all-round, but soon changed to hydraulic operation and eventually to all-wheel discs.

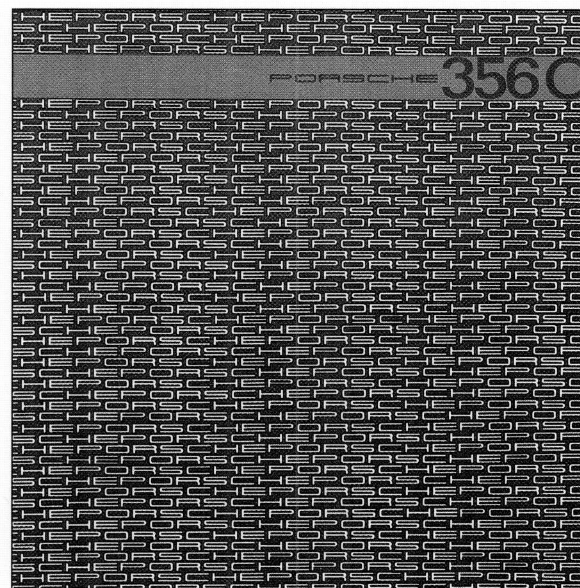

PORSCH

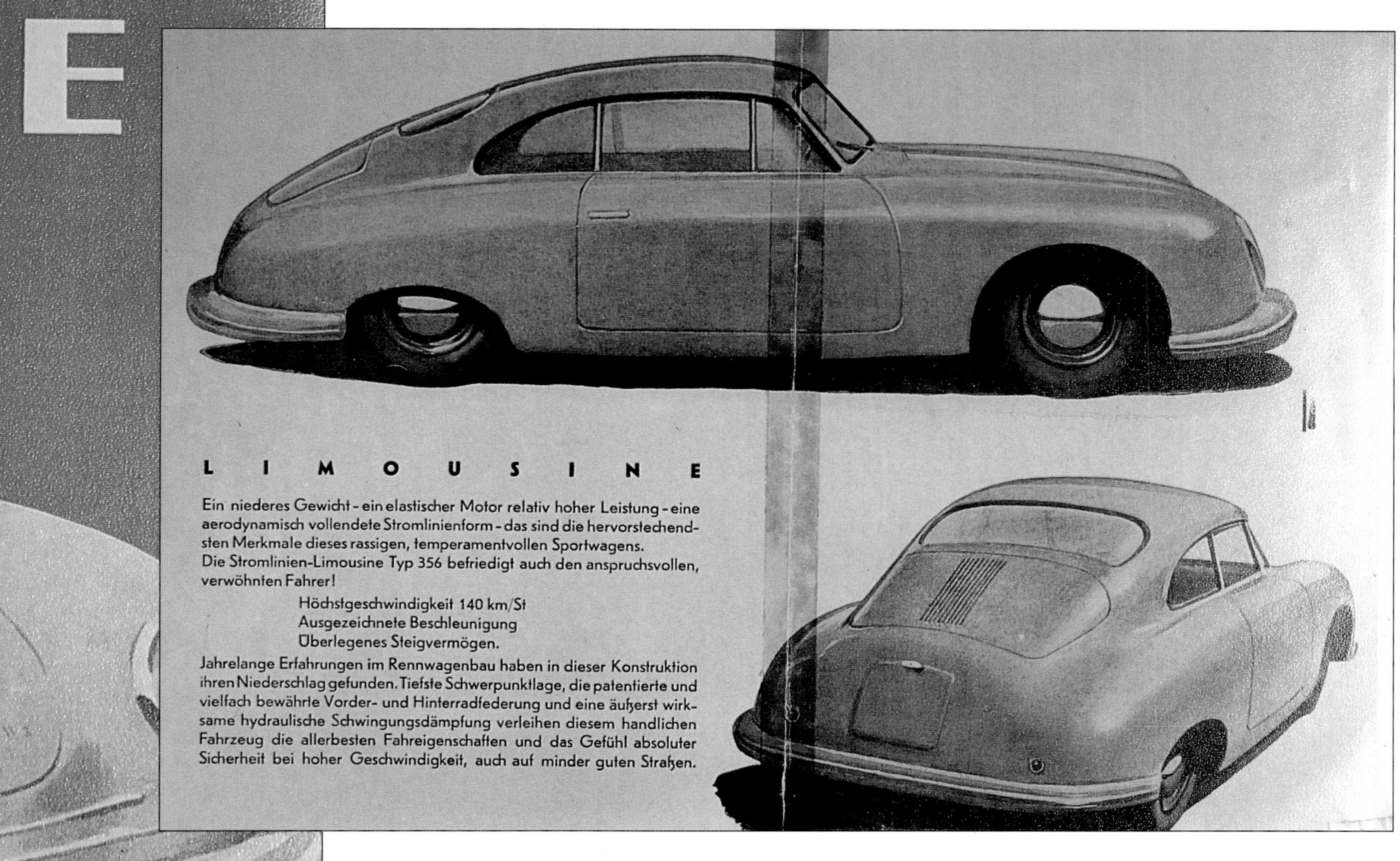

L I M O U S I N E

Ein niederes Gewicht - ein elastischer Motor relativ hoher Leistung - eine aerodynamisch vollendete Stromlinienform - das sind die hervorstechendsten Merkmale dieses rassigen, temperamentvollen Sportwagens.
Die Stromlinien-Limousine Typ 356 befriedigt auch den anspruchsvollen, verwöhnten Fahrer!

Höchstgeschwindigkeit 140 km/St
Ausgezeichnete Beschleunigung
Überlegenes Steigvermögen.

Jahrelange Erfahrungen im Rennwagenbau haben in dieser Konstruktion ihren Niederschlag gefunden. Tiefste Schwerpunktlage, die patentierte und vielfach bewährte Vorder- und Hinterradfederung und eine äußerst wirksame hydraulische Schwingungsdämpfung verleihen diesem handlichen Fahrzeug die allerbesten Fahreigenschaften und das Gefühl absoluter Sicherheit bei hoher Geschwindigkeit, auch auf minder guten Straßen.

LEFT, 1948: *Designated 356/2, the first production Porsches (356/1 was the one and only prototype) used many mechanical parts from the Volkswagen Beetle. However the power output was increased by 60 per cent and this, combined with the light weight and slippery shape, enabled the cars to reach top speeds of 90mph (140kph). Externally, these early cars were the only ones to feature an aluminium trim around and to each side of the front licence plate. They also had two-piece flat windscreens with vertically-parking wipers.*

ABOVE, 1948: *The interior featured bucket seats and instrumentation consisting of a speedometer and little else. Production began in Gmünd, Austria and after two years a total of only 51 cars had been built.*

ABOVE, 1951: *In 1950, Porsche moved back to its pre-war home of Stuttgart. By the following year production had risen to 60 cars a month and the 1,000th Porsche rolled off the production line at the end of August 1951.*

LEFT, 1951: *Early in 1951, a bored-out 1300cc version of the original engine was introduced producing 44bhp. Later the same year a redesigned 1500cc unit became the top option. This featured roller bearings to reduce friction and increase reliability. Aluminium cylinder heads replaced the previous cast iron type, and larger Solex carburettors were added. Power output was 60bhp and top speed rose to 96mph (150kph). To cope with the extra power, twin leading-shoe hydraulic brakes were added and telescopic dampers replaced the lever-arm units at the rear.*

LEFT, 1951: *The bodywork was revised in several minor ways and was now made of steel for ease of production. The flat two-piece windscreen was retained, but the side windows became one-piece.*

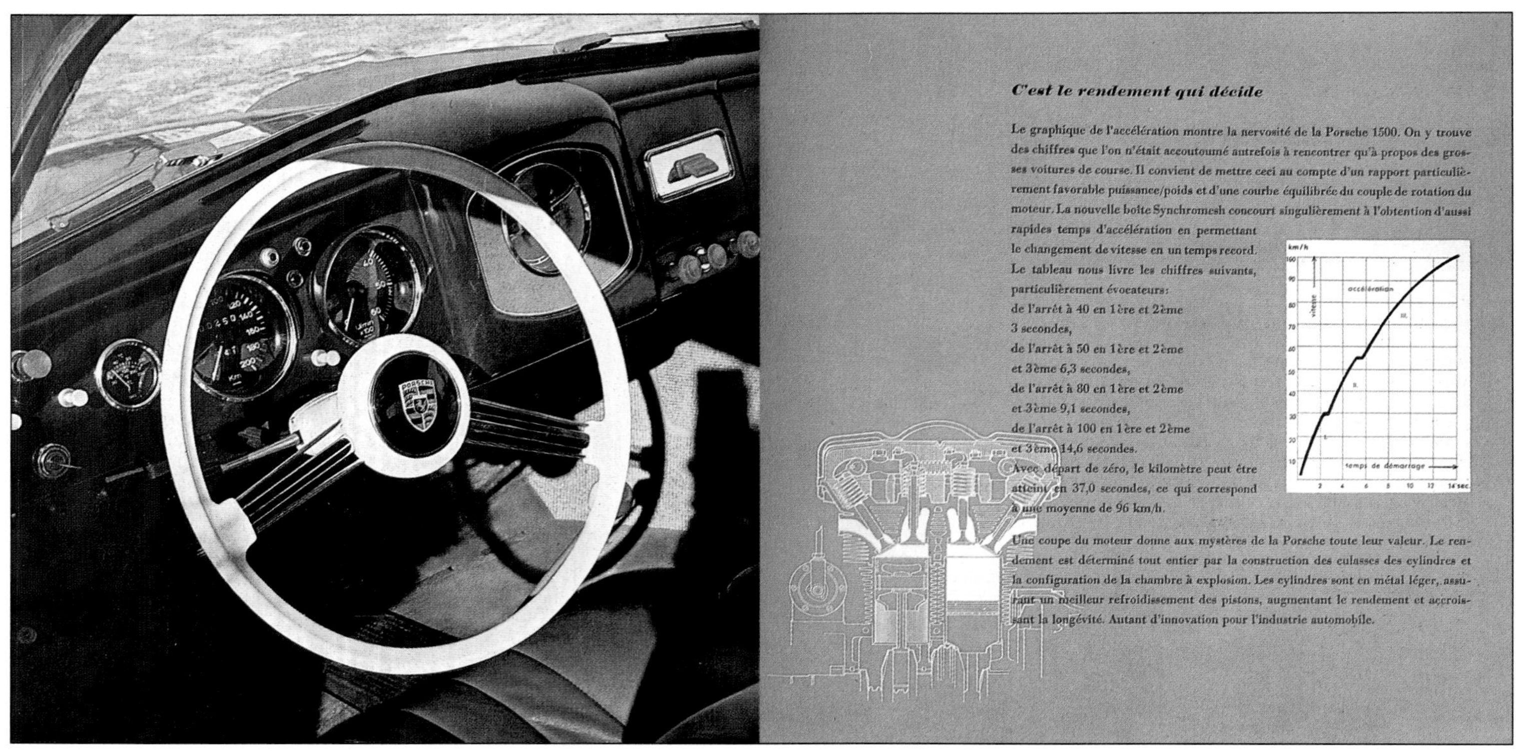

C'est le rendement qui décide

Le graphique de l'accélération montre la nervosité de la Porsche 1500. On y trouve des chiffres que l'on n'était accoutoumé autrefois à rencontrer qu'à propos des grosses voitures de course. Il convient de mettre ceci au compte d'un rapport particulièrement favorable puissance/poids et d'une courbe équilibrée du couple de rotation du moteur. La nouvelle boite Synchromesh concourt singulièrement à l'obtention d'aussi rapides temps d'accélération en permettant le changement de vitesse en un temps record. Le tableau nous livre les chiffres suivants, particulièrement évocateurs:
de l'arrêt à 40 en 1ère et 2ème
3 secondes,
de l'arrêt à 50 en 1ère et 2ème
et 3ème 6,3 secondes,
de l'arrêt à 80 en 1ère et 2ème
et 3ème 9,1 secondes,
de l'arrêt à 100 en 1ère et 2ème
et 3ème 14,6 secondes.
Avec départ de zéro, le kilomètre peut être atteint en 37,0 secondes, ce qui correspond à une moyenne de 96 km/h.

Une coupe du moteur donne aux mystères de la Porsche toute leur valeur. Le rendement est déterminé tout entier par la construction des culasses des cylindres et la configuration de la chambre à explosion. Les cylindres sont en métal léger, assurant un meilleur refroidissement des pistons, augmentant le rendement et accroissant la longévité. Autant d'innovation pour l'industrie automobile.

LEFT, 1953: *The car's design continued to be refined, and in 1952 acquired a one-piece windscreen, although still V-shaped. This was also the year when the Porsche emblem was introduced. The interior was refined, the dashboard now featuring a tachometer, clock and fuel gauge, with a radio as an optional extra. Reclining seatbacks were added and the rear seats could be folded down.*

LEFT, 1953: *Mechanically, the main change in 1952 was the introduction of a new, all-synchromesh gearbox. This eliminated one early criticism of the design, and motoring journalists began to write in quite glowing terms about the cars, citing the build quality, gear change and lack of wind noise amongst the plus points. The handling of the car was, however, a more controversial point. It was generally agreed that, in the hands of a skilful or expert driver, the car could be driven very quickly indeed. But it could also get a lesser driver into trouble more quickly than anything else on the road at the time.*

LEFT, 1953: *Also in 1954, the 1500S was introduced with an engine developing 70bhp, nearly three times the original unit. Maximum speed of this new model was 105mph (approx 168kph), and the 0–60 acceleration time was around 10 seconds. For 1955, some modifications were made to the front suspension, including the addition of an anti-roll bar. Minor cosmetic changes were also made to items such as door handles, and windscreen washers became standard equipment. Inside, the heater controls moved from the dashboard to the floor tunnel, and a trip meter was added to the speedo.*

RIGHT, 1953: *Because of the car's temperamental handling, Porsche salesmen would recommend their customers to take a few thousand miles to become accustomed to the car. 1953 saw minor improvements, mainly to the soundproofing, and a roller-bearing version of the 1300cc engine was introduced as the 1300S. In March 1954 the 5,000th car rolled out of Zuffenhausen.*

ABOVE, 1960: *Although used in French brochures as late as the early 1960s, these pictures show Porsche's new 356A, which was introduced in 1956. At first glance there appeared to be little change in the 1956 models, but closer examination and the new designation of 356A revealed a major overhaul of the design, including changes to engines, suspension and dashboard.*

ABOVE, 1962: *The most obvious external differences included the curved windscreen and the reduction in wheel size to 15 inches (37cm), which allowed the fitment of wider tyres. This, together with a number of minor suspension and chassis modifications, gave the car a slightly softer ride with greatly improved handling. The 1500cc engines were enlarged to 1600cc, and a new transmission was fitted. The dashboard was changed to a flat panel incorporating speedometer, tachometer and a combined fuel/ temperature gauge.*

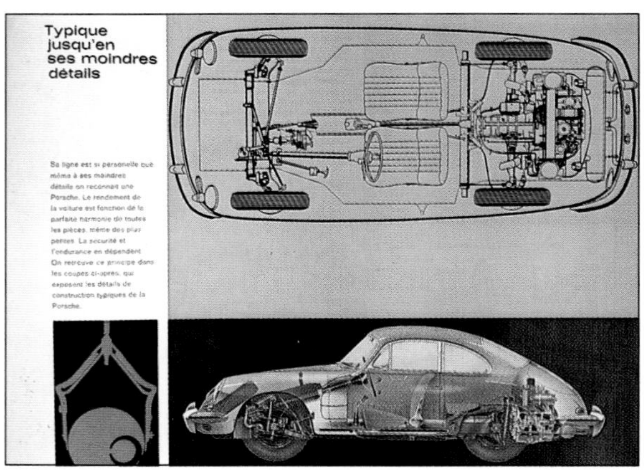

ABOVE, 1963: *All these modifications combined to give far more flexibility to the top 1600cc models. They also significantly improved the handling, giving the car less of a rear-engine feel.*

RIGHT, 1961: *This brochure, which compares the 356A (left) with its successor the 356B, shows the one-piece 'tear-drop' shaped tail lights, which replaced the twin round units in 1957. Padded sunvisors were now standard and the speedometer was relocated. In 1958, both 1300cc engines were dropped, and the 1600cc pushrod engines reverted to plain bearings. The normal 1600 also reverted to cast-iron cylinder blocks to reduce both noise and production cost. A new ZF steering box was used and the steering wheel was enlarged to 16.75 inches (50cm) in diameter to further reduce steering effort.*

RIGHT, 1960: *External changes included the repositioning of the exhaust pipes to align the tips with the lower part of the rear bumper over-riders. This improved the rear ground clearance, but also made the bumpers dirtier. The Porsche crest was incorporated into the centre of the hubcaps and the wheel embellishers were changed to a more slotted pattern. Improved door locks were fitted and the door handle design was again subtly changed. By the end of its production run in late 1959, the 356A had changed considerably from the previous model. In fact, some motoring journalists were amazed how such comprehensive changes could be made to a design so unobtrusively.*

BELOW, 1960: *The introduction of the 356B in 1960 marked a radical redesign of the car. In fact, the new car came as something of a culture shock to some 'Porschephiles' used to quiet progression. Some went as far as accusing the company of 'doing a Detroit', but most already realized that there was a good reason for every change that Porsche made.*

ABOVE, 1961: *Rear seats were redesigned to give better headroom, and the folding seat back was split to give greater versatility. Ventilation was improved and opening quarter vents were reintroduced in the side windows. Engine size remained at 1600cc and a new 90bhp variant was added, designated Super 90. An enlarged-capacity oil pump was fitted to all engines. There were now no models with a top speed below 100mph (160kph). Brakes were further improved with the addition of new finned aluminium drums and the addition of a backplate seal to help keep water out of the drums.*

LEFT, 1960: *The whole front end was redesigned with revised bonnet shape. A new front bumper with larger over-riders was added, and both front and rear bumper heights were raised by 4 inches for added protection from parking incidents. The front trafficators were more bulbous, and additional brake cooling vents were cut in the front valence below the bumper.*

LEFT, 1963: *In 1962, the body styling was further revised to incorporate a larger windscreen and rear window. There were two intake grilles on the engine cover. The fuel filler cap was moved outside under a flap on the top of the right front wing. The fuel tank was redesigned to provide more luggage space under the bonnet. The battery was relocated and the fuse panel moved from inside the car to the front luggage compartment. Fresh-air ventilation was greatly improved with the addition of a vent ahead of the windscreen which fed air into a new controllable distribution system to outlets above and below the dashboard. Also in 1962, a curious fixed hardtop body style was introduced, this being manufactured by Karmann. This was similar in appearance to a cabriolet fitted with the removable hardtop. It did not prove popular and only sold in small numbers. Overall, the 356B was numerically the most popular of the 356 series, with over 30,000 built during its four-year production run.*

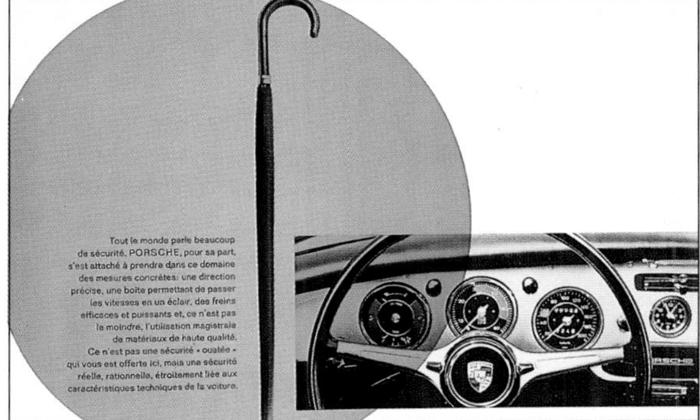

RIGHT, 1962: *So dramatic were the improvements that testers were now reporting that the handling was so good that only 'the most hapless, witless or inept driver could let the car get away from him'. There were still criticisms, but these were now mainly aesthetic and the overwhelming impression was that of a thoroughly sorted, reliable and above all rewarding machine.*

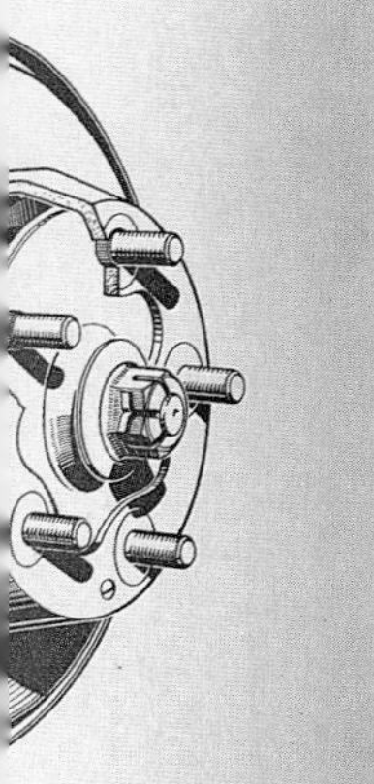

elf-adjusting devices in the design in the car, is the expanding lever type, has

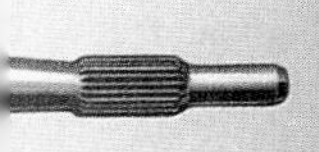

amous Porsche-patent ring design. A great part of the erience of manipulating the ooth and precisely through

When motor enthusiasts talk shop, about compact, high performance, air-cooled engines, they'll always come round to the Porsche . . . the most successful post-war German sports car. Aside from the 2-liter Carrera (4 cylinders) and the newly conceived 901 (6 cylinders), the bulk of Porsche production is still concentrated on the 1600 cc flat four engine.

The 356 C version, available in a choice of either 75 or 95 hp DIN, has the same general layout as its predecessors, with overhead valves controlled, via pushrods and rocker arms, by the crankcase-mounted camshaft. In detail, however, the engine has been further refined. A new cylinder head with improved intake and exhaust channeling, provides greatly increased flexibility in performance, especially in the torque ranges. The Super or SC engine has had its horsepower boosted from 90 to 95 DIN.

The Cabriolet with soft top

ABOVE, 1963/64: *Introduced midway through 1963, the 356C was the final production model of the series. Visually it was virtually identical to the last of the 'B' models except for further enlargement of the rear window and a new design of wheels and hubcaps. The reason for the latter was the major mechanical change to the car, the introduction of disc brakes on all four wheels, a first for a standard Porsche production car.*

ABOVE, 1963/4: *The 356C was the most highly developed of the standard road cars, and was well received by the motoring press. Only that small carping minority of journalists who forever criticize for criticism's sake had anything negative to say about it, yet even these comments were restricted to what in their opinion amounted to 'needless cost-cutting'.*

RIGHT, 1963–65: *For five years, Porsche had been experimenting with two different types of disc brake, one from Dunlop and the other of their own design. They finally settled on the Dunlop system, but added some facets of their own system, particularly the separate hand brake working on a small diameter drum incorporated inside the rear discs. Just two engines were now offered, 1600C and 1600SC, these being developments of the 1600S and Super 90 respectively.*

Coupé

The Coupe, a two-seater with two occasional seats (changeable into luggage space) has long been the favorite Porsche body. Classic in line, the original Coupe shape was the product of aerodynamic design and engineering... an extension and modernization of the horsecarriage concept of a solid top on a closed body. The Porsche Coupe today embodies many improvements and refinements in engineering and styling; windows have been enlarged for greater visibility; controlled air intake provides better ventilation, seating has been made more comfortable. Basically, however, the design remains unchanged... harmonious, aesthetically pleasing, timeless.

ABOVE, 1964: *When production finally ceased in 1965, over 76,000 356s had been produced in the 15 years since the return to Zuffenhausen. The car had set the company on its way in terms of production, and had made the company wealthy enough to embark upon the design of a replacement, a car which would become an all-time classic, the 911.*

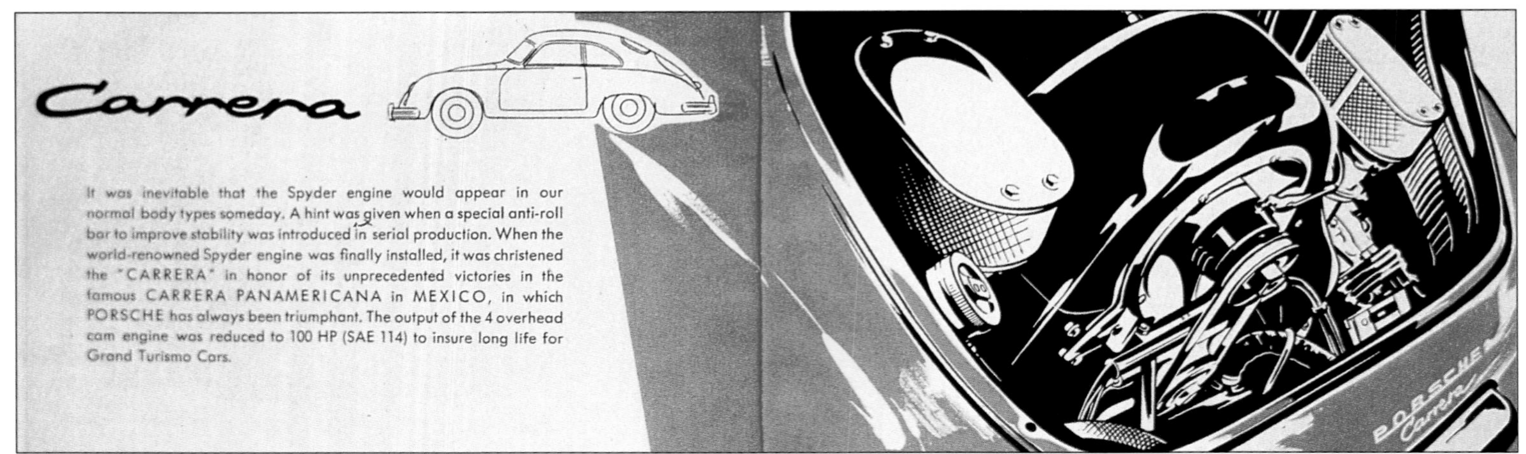

Carrera

It was inevitable that the Spyder engine would appear in our normal body types someday. A hint was given when a special anti-roll bar to improve stability was introduced in serial production. When the world-renowned Spyder engine was finally installed, it was christened the "CARRERA" in honor of its unprecedented victories in the famous CARRERA PANAMERICANA in MEXICO, in which PORSCHE has always been triumphant. The output of the 4 overhead cam engine was reduced to 100 HP (SAE 114) to insure long life for Grand Turismo Cars.

ABOVE, 1955–57: *During the 15-year run of the 356, there were several models introduced with either alternative body styles or equipment. One of these was the Carrera, basically an uprated sporting package. Early in 1952, Porsche engineers embarked on the development of a racing version of the 1500cc engine. This culminated a year later in a revised design featuring twin overhead camshafts on each bank of cylinders, dual twin-choke carburettors, dual ignition and dry-sump lubrication. The result was 110bhp which, when fitted in a 550 Spyder, performed impressively in the Mexican Carrera Panamerica road race.*

BOTTOM LEFT, 1955: *In 1955, a slightly detuned 100bhp version of the engine was fitted in a coupe for trials and this was developed into a road version, introduced with the new 356A models in 1956 and designated the 1500GS 'Carrera', after the race where the engine scored its first success.*

RIGHT, 1957: *Externally, the only distinguishing features of the early cars were the gold 'Carrera' script badges on the front wings and engine cover, plus twin exhausts. Two models were offered, the deluxe and GT, the latter being a stripped version with plastic windows, aluminium doors, bonnet and engine cover and Spyder front brakes. From late 1958, GS engines reverted to plain bearings. In 1959 the 1600GS was introduced, but this was a fairly luxurious model and therefore somewhat heavier than the earlier versions.*

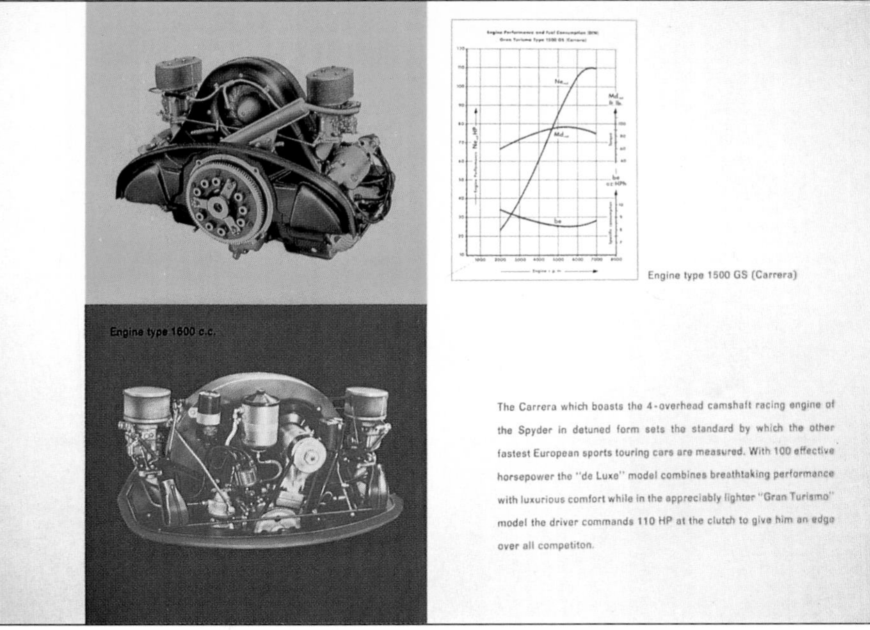

Engine type 1600 c.c.

Engine type 1500 GS (Carrera)

The Carrera which boasts the 4-overhead camshaft racing engine of the Spyder in detuned form sets the standard by which the other fastest European sports touring cars are measured. With 100 effective horsepower the "de Luxe" model combines breathtaking performance with luxurious comfort while in the appreciably lighter "Gran Turismo" model the driver commands 110 HP at the clutch to give him an edge over all competiton.

ABOVE, 1960: *So, in 1960, Porsche entered into an agreement with Zagato and Abarth to produce a new lightweight version which became the Abarth Carrera GTL, with distinctive special streamlined bodywork. Only around 20 of these cars were built, most of which were purchased for competition use. The type scored many successes including class wins at Le Mans. This car was further developed through the 2000GS/GT to culminate in the 904 series of racing variants.*

RIGHT, 1951: *The Cabriolet was an alternative body style offered right through the entire production life of the 356 models. It was effectively a convertible version of the basic coupe. It should, therefore, not be confused with the Speedster model and its derivatives, which had an entirely different body designed by Reutters and is featured on pages 38 and 39.*

RIGHT, 1953: *The Cabriolet incorporated a fully padded hood and framed wind-up side windows. The hood folded neatly onto the back of the car when not in use, and a tailored cover was provided to tidy up the appearance. Because of the close links to the basic coupe, modifications and changes of model were incorporated on the Cabriolets at the same time as the basic coupes.*

PORSCHE CABRIOLET

Typ 356

Das Porsche-Cabriolet ist der exklusive Sportwagen, gleichsam das Dior-Modell aus der Porsche-Familie.

Ob in Paris oder San Francisco, in Casablanca oder Meran – es gibt kaum eine Schönheitskonkurrenz, wo Porsche-Wagen nicht mit den höchsten Auszeichnungen dekoriert werden. Aber man soll über der Harmonie und Eleganz der äußeren Form die inneren Vorzüge nicht vergessen:

Sparsamkeit, Sicherheit und Höchstgeschwindigkeit vereinigen sich zu einem Dreiklang des Fortschritts. Straßenlage und Beschleunigung sind die eines Rennwagens – daher die Sicherheit im Verkehr. Kraftreserve und Fahrkomfort entsprechen dem höchsten europäischen Standard.

Bestechend in seiner äußeren Form, die sowohl der Forderung nach Windschlüpfrigkeit als auch den ästhetischen Wünschen der verwöhntesten Kunden gerecht wird.

Ein für einen Sportwagen unvergleichlicher **Fahrkomfort.**

Infolge der guten Stahlisolierung geräuscharm. Bequeme zweifach verstellbare Sitze. Spielend leicht zu bedienen; geringer Kraftaufwand bei Lenkung und Schaltung.

Anspruchslos im Betrieb. Einfache Pflege und Wartung. Luftgekühlt. Startfreudig auch bei grimmiger Kälte.

Technische Daten:

Motor-Typ	1300 A	1300 S	1500	1500 S
Bauart	4-Zylinder-Boxer-Motor, luftgekühlt	4-Zylinder-Boxer-Motor, luftgekühlt	4-Zylinder-Boxer-Motor, luftgekühlt	4-Zylinder-Boxer-Motor, luftgekühlt
Zylinder-Bohrung	74,5	74,5	80	80
Kolbenhub	74	74	74	74
Hubraum	1290	1290	1488	1488
Leistung	44 PS bei 4200 U/min	60 PS bei 5500 U/min	55 PS bei 4400 U/min	70 PS bei 5000 U/min
Höchstgeschwindigkeit	145 km/h	160 km/h	155 km/h	170 km/h
Kraftstoff-Normverbrauch	6,7 Ltr./100 km	7,5 Ltr./100 km	7,3 Ltr./100 km	7,8 Ltr./100 km
Fahrgestell	**1300 A**	**1300 S**	**1500**	**1500 S**
Länge	3950 mm	3950 mm	3950 mm	3950 mm
Breite	1660 mm	1660 mm	1660 mm	1660 mm
Höhe	1300 mm	1300 mm	1300 mm	1300 mm

Änderungen vorbehalten

Have you ever driven an open car? Of course, the ladies must wear a scarf and there is more wind noise than in a closed car. On the other hand, one feels more intimate with the elements of nature and will find car driving more of a sport with wind, sun, and the sky all around. Have you ever taken a close look at the Porsche convertible top? Here is one convertible top still from the old school – solid and tough – and even the worst of downpours can't budge it. Opening and closing isn't even a problem for ladies. The important thing about it is that even with the top up one still can see out. The rear window is large and can be opened by a pull on the zipper. As you can see, Porsche gives much consideration to the little things.

Cabriolet

Cabriolet
D'une grande beauté,
le cabriolet,
avec son aménagement
intérieur des plus complets
aux teintes d'harmonisant
parfaitement, offre un
confort qui ne laisse rien
à désirer. Grâce à sa
capote facile à fermer,
cette voiture présente,
en hiver,
tous les avantages
d'un élégant
coupé deux tons.

Dans les virages, le ressort de compensation sur le pont arrière pousse sur le sol la roue la moins chargée, intérieure au tournant, avec la force de la roue extérieure chargée.

ABOVE, 1955: *The first Cabriolets were built by Beutlers in Berne, Switzerland and based on the 356/2 Gmünd-built cars. In 1950, Cabriolet production was moved to Reutters, and the first of their examples began to appear in late 1950. The only obvious external differences were that the nameplate was moved to a position on the front panel just below the lid.*

RIGHT, 1961: *When the one-piece V-screen was fitted in 1952, a thin chrome rod had to be bolted centrally between the dashboard and the top of the screen frame to support the interior rear view mirror. Even with the later changes, this feature was retained right through to the last 356C Cabriolets as shown by this 1961 brochure. In 1958, a larger rear window improved poor rear visibility in the Cabriolet with the hood in the raised position. At the same time, opening quarter vents were incorporated into the side windows for improved hood-up ventilation.*

ABOVE, 1964: *The Cabriolet was always considered as one of the better convertible-top cars available at the time. The hood was easy to open and close single-handed, and the padded design made the car almost as quiet with the hood up as the normal coupe. For owners living in less friendly climates, a factory hardtop was available, manufactured for Porsche by Brendel. This gave a distinctive notchback appearance which obviously influenced the styling of the Karmann-built 356Bs mentioned earlier.*

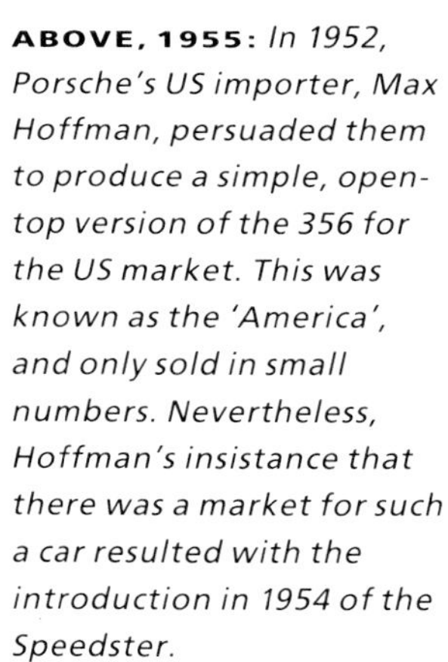

ABOVE, 1955: *In 1952, Porsche's US importer, Max Hoffman, persuaded them to produce a simple, open-top version of the 356 for the US market. This was known as the 'America', and only sold in small numbers. Nevertheless, Hoffman's insistance that there was a market for such a car resulted with the introduction in 1954 of the Speedster.*

BELOW, 1955: *This was in effect a Cabriolet produced down to a price which Hoffman had set as the maximum that the US market would pay for such a car. He had got his arithmetic exactly right and the car was an instant success, helping total 1955 production of 356s to reach nearly 3,000 cars.*

Gestern noch ein Zukunftstraum ..

Der Speedster ist sozusagen das Sonntagskind der internationalen Automobiltechnik. Er ist leichter als Coupé und Cabriolet, noch rassiger in seiner Linienführung und für sonnige Tage der Wagen, den sich alle Glückspilze wünschen. Will man ihn genauer charakterisieren, so könnte man ihn den klassischen Sportwagen der großen europäischen Schule nennen. Der Form nach ist er der Traumwagen von morgen. Pantherhaft geduckt – als könnte er jeden Augenblick zu einem machtvollen Sprung ansetzen – steht er da. Die Straßenlage ist so ideal, daß man auch bei Spitzengeschwindigkeiten nie das Gefühl der Sicherheit verliert. Der Fahrersitz befindet sich genau im Schwerpunkt. Der Heckmotor ist – wie bei den andern Porsche-Wagen – luftgekühlt. Professor Porsche hat seinen ersten luftgekühlten Motor schon 1912 gebaut. Kein Wunder also, daß in den Porsche-Motoren zahlreiche Erkenntnisse und Erfahrungen verwirklicht wurden, die vor allem der Lebensdauer des Motors zugute kommen.

TECHNISCHE DATEN

Motor	1500	1500 S (Super)
Bauart	4-Zylinder-Boxer-Motor, luftgekühlt	4-Zylinder-Boxer-Motor, luftgekühlt
Zylinder-Bohrung	80 mm	80 mm
Kolbenhub	74 mm	74 mm
Hubraum	1488 cm³	1488 cm³
Leistung	55 PS bei 4400 U/min.	70 PS bei 5000 U/min.
Höchstgeschwindigkeit	155 km/h	170 km/h
Kraftstoff-Normverbrauch	7,4 Ltr./100 km	7,9 Ltr./100 km
Fahrgestell	**1500**	**1500 S (Super)**
Länge	3950 mm	3950 mm
Breite	1660 mm	1660 mm
Höhe (mit Verdeck)	1220 mm	1220 mm
Änderungen vorbehalten		

DR.-ING. h. c. F. PORSCHE K.-G. · STUTTGART-ZUFFENHAUSEN

ABOVE, 1955: *The body was designed and built by Reutters and had a more cut-down appearance than the Cabriolet although, from the waistline down, it was identical to the Cabriolet. It was the windscreen, 3.5 inches (9cm) shorter than the one in the Cabriolet and supported in a thin chromed frame, that gave the car its lower look. This was helped by the addition of a full-length chrome strip on each side passing through the line of the door handles. The hood was a much simpler affair and made the interior somewhat claustrophobic for tall drivers when in the raised position.*

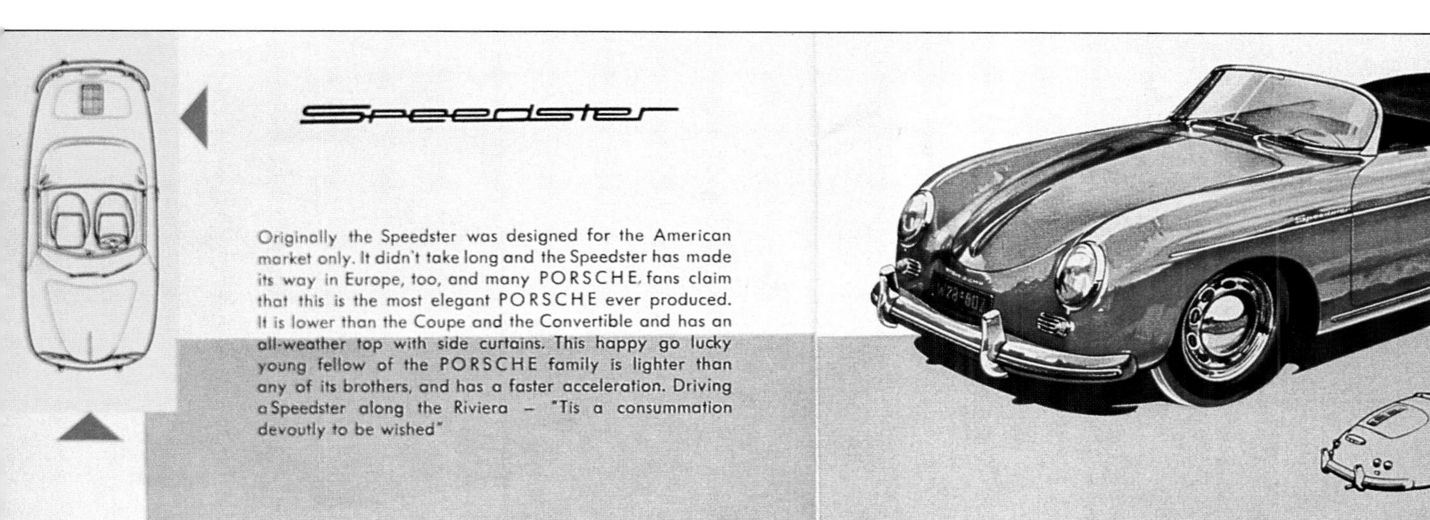

LEFT, 1955: *The replacement for the Speedster was originally designated 'Speedster D' because it was to be built by a new sub-contractor Drauz of Heilbronn. However, shortly before introduction it was rechristened the 'Convertible D'. It featured a slightly taller windscreen and a less basic hood design, something of a cross between the original design and the luxury padded version on the Cabriolet. Wind-up windows were included, but the distinctive Speedster dashboard was retained, as were the chrome body strips.*

ABOVE, 1955: *In 1960, with the introduction of the 356B models, the Convertible D became the Roadster, a title it was to retain to the end of its production run in 1963. Drauz were joined by a Belgian company called D'Leteren as producers of the Roadster bodies. Carrera variants were also produced in Speedster or Roadster bodies, but these were generally the GT variant, stripped even further of equipment, and were mainly used for competition purposes.*

RIGHT, 1956: *The 550 Spyders were the ultimate development of the 356 design and were intended as out-and-out competition machines. Two of the cars competed in the Carrera Panamericana race in Mexico in 1953 and finished first and second in their class. In 1954 on its debut in the Mille Miglia, a gruelling 1000 mile road race around Italy, the 550 finished sixth overall, and took the 1500cc class win. For the four years it was entered, from 1954 to 1957, the 550RS took the 1500cc class win at Le Mans, finishing in overall positions of 12th, 4th, 5th and 8th respectively. Many other prizes were won and the 550 set the tone for all of the special competition models to follow over the years.*

LEFT, 1955: *Customer versions of the car were known as the 550A/1500RS, and the majority were purchased for serious racing. A few, however, were used as road cars, and probably the most famous of these was one with the rather distinctive California license plate 'L'il Bastard' owned by the legendary James Dean.*

Some day, all convertibles will have a roll bar.

At last. The basic problem of open car safety has been solved. With a roll bar fully integrated into the total design of the car.

The new Porsche Targa is the first production-series convertible to have it. Like all Porsches, the distinctive new Targa is rugged, racing-inspired and designed to be driven hard and fast—with maximum safety.

For years, roll bars have been standard equipment on all open racing cars. In the Targa—appropriately named for the punishing Sicilian mountain road race that's become one of Porsche's most successful proving grounds—the built-in roll bar provides race-track protection for everyday driving. It also separates top and back, so you can use either part without the other, if you wish. Porsche offers the Targa in three versions, each with the same engine and equipment as the corresponding Porsche coupe: the 912, 911 and 911L.

LEFT, 1967: *The competition successes were still considered significant enough for Porsche to use pictures of both the Spyder and the Speedster (pictured here) nearly ten years later in promotional material for the then new Targa-bodied 911 models.*

911

There is no doubt that the 911 is the one model which epitomizes the Porsche tradition. To a lot of enthusiasts, there simply is no other true Porsche. This is not as surprising as it sounds, because the 911 has been a current model for no less than 65 per cent of the company's production history. True, it has been written-off more than a few times over this timescale by many pundits who have described it as old-fashioned, over-priced, a classic after its time, and so on. But regardless, it endures and evolves, the ultimate automotive survivor. Perhaps all that remains to be added to the design is a small bumper sticker which would read 'As you can see, rumours of my death have been greatly exaggerated'.

Work started on the replacement for the 356 in 1959. 'Butzi' Porsche created a new body style which would be only 6 inches (15cm) longer than the 356 and 2 inches (5cm) narrower. Over the years this would develop through various stages into a turbocharged unit with a capacity of 3.3 litres and producing 320bhp in road trim. Over the years this would develop through various stages into a turbocharged unit with a capacity of 3.3 litres and producing 320bhp in road trim. There would also be various racing versions including the 935/78 cars, nicknamed 'Moby Dick' because of their elongated whale-shaped bodywork. The engines in these cars produced an incredible 845bhp assisted by a number of racing modifications to what was still a 930 Turbo engine.

A new 6-cylinder unit was designed by Ferdinand Piech and developed by Hans Tomala. This new design still utilized the horizontally-opposed cylinder arrangement and began with a capacity of 1991cc producing 130bhp.

The new body was prepared for production by Erwin Komenda, who 15 years earlier, had performed the same task on the original 356. At the same time a second body variant appeared, the Targa, which has always been a popular model and remains in production today. The first changes appeared in 1969 when the wings became mildly flared to accommodate wider wheels which were necessary to handle the increasing power output. The first major restyling arrived in 1974 with the introduction of new bumpers to meet the increasingly stringent US safety regulations. This was followed by the Turbo variants which sported exaggerated wing flares and a large tail spoiler.

When the 911SC was introduced in 1978, the main external differences were further flaring of the rear wheelarches, wider than the standard 2.7-litre cars, but narrower than the Turbo, and colour-keyed headlamp rims instead of the previous chrome type. Little changed when the cars were renamed 'Carrera' again in 1982, except for the long-overdue addition of a Cabriolet model to the range. 1988 brought the Carrera 2, the most radical change since 1974. The car was given a more 'nineties' look, with the restyling of the nose into a one-piece composite bumper panel with the indicators, sidelights and fog lights amalgamated into one large wrap-around unit on either side.

A 3.6-litre engine was used along with a retractable spoiler. A new 'Tiptronic' transmission gave a clutchless four-speed manual change with the option of fully-automatic selection. A full-time four-wheel drive variant was offered as the Carrera 4. Thus, the 911 continues to be more upwardly-mobile than some of its erstwhile owners.

ABOVE, 1963: *First shown at Frankfurt in 1963, the new Porsche was designated the 901. However, because of a potential clash with the Peugeot model numbering system, this was changed to 911 before production commenced in 1964.*

LEFT AND BELOW, 1963: *The new car met all of the design criteria set out by Ferry Porsche four years earlier. It had more interior space, whilst remaining only marginally larger externally than the 356, to which it carried a firm family resemblance. It was more powerful, more comfortable, quieter and smoother than the old car and much easier to handle. New features included a 6-cylinder engine, dry-sump lubrication, MacPherson Strut front suspension, semi-trailing arm rear suspension, rack and pinion steering and 12-volt electrical system.*

RIGHT, 1966: *There is an old engineering adage which states that if a machine looks right, then more often than not it is right. Although this would not be a fitting premise with which to embark on any project, it holds good with cars like the 911. The design was so obviously right from day one that it has endured 27 further years of development which have changed its specification out of all recognition without changing its character recognizably. In true Porsche tradition the 911 constantly evolved, some of the modifications coming as a result of customer complaints. One of these, perceived excessive understeer and front-end 'float', was cured in an ingenious way by fitting cast-iron weights inside the front bumper end plates. In fact, the majority of owners who received this modification drove away from the factory, much impressed by their better handling car, yet blissfully unaware of how basic the modification had been. Subsequent production modifications totally cured this problem on later cars, of course.*

RIGHT, 1966: *In 1965, the Targa variant was added to the range. This was an open-topped 911 without the canvas hood. Instead, a solid roll-over bar was fitted behind the door, and the space between this and the windscreen was filled with a one-piece lift-out panel. The rear window initially comprised a zip-out transparent panel, but this proved troublesome and was ultimately replaced with a fixed glass screen. The result of this unusual arrangement was a best of both worlds situation where true open-air motoring could be enjoyed, whilst hood-up motoring could be as quiet and comfortable as a normal coupe or hardtop.*

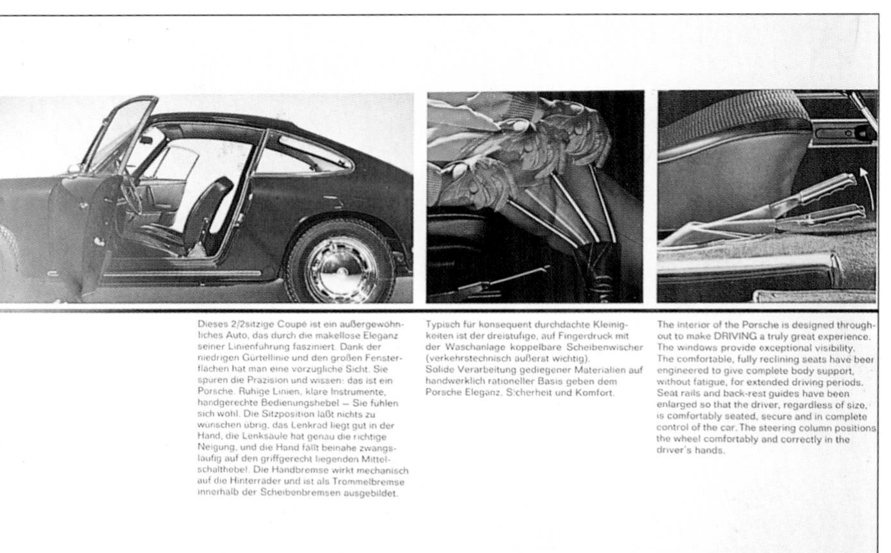

Dieses 2/2sitzige Coupé ist ein außergewöhnliches Auto, das durch die makellose Eleganz seiner Linienführung fasziniert. Dank der niedrigen Gürtellinie und den großen Fensterflächen hat man eine vorzügliche Sicht. Sie spüren die Präzision und wissen: das ist ein Porsche. Ruhige Linien, klare Instrumente, handgerechte Bedienungshebel – Sie fühlen sich wohl. Die Sitzposition läßt nichts zu wünschen übrig, das Lenkrad liegt gut in der Hand, die Lenksäule hat genau die richtige Neigung, und die Hand fällt beinahe zwangsläufig auf den griffgerecht liegenden Mittelschalthebel. Die Handbremse wirkt mechanisch auf die Hinterräder und ist als Trommelbremse innerhalb der Scheibenbremsen ausgebildet.

Typisch für konsequent durchdachte Kleinigkeiten ist der dreistufige, auf Fingerdruck mit der Waschanlage koppelbare Scheibenwischer (verkehrstechnisch äußerst wichtig).
Solide Verarbeitung gediegener Materialien auf handwerklich rationeller Basis geben dem Porsche Eleganz, Sicherheit und Komfort.

The interior of the Porsche is designed throughout to make DRIVING a truly great experience. The windows provide exceptional visibility. The comfortable, fully reclining seats have been engineered to give complete body support, without fatigue, for extended driving periods. Seat rails and back-rest guides have been enlarged so that the driver, regardless of size, is comfortably seated, secure and in complete control of the car. The steering column positions the wheel comfortably and correctly in the driver's hands.

Bedienungs- und Fahrkomfort

The Porsche is designed for DRIVING . . .

LEFT, 1966: *Needless to say, the variant has proved very popular over the years, giving improved rearward vision. Porsche also retained, for a while, a 4-cylinder version of the car called the 912. This was a basic 911 fitted with the old 1600SC engine from the 356, and provided a cheaper-priced alternative to the 6-cylinder cars which were already moving up-market.*

RIGHT and FAR RIGHT, 1967: *In 1967 a new higher-performance variant, the 911S, was introduced. Engine modifications included new camshafts, larger valves, improved cylinder heads with higher compression ratio, and Weber carburettors. All of this increased the power output by over 20 per cent to 160bhp.*

Particolari tecnici

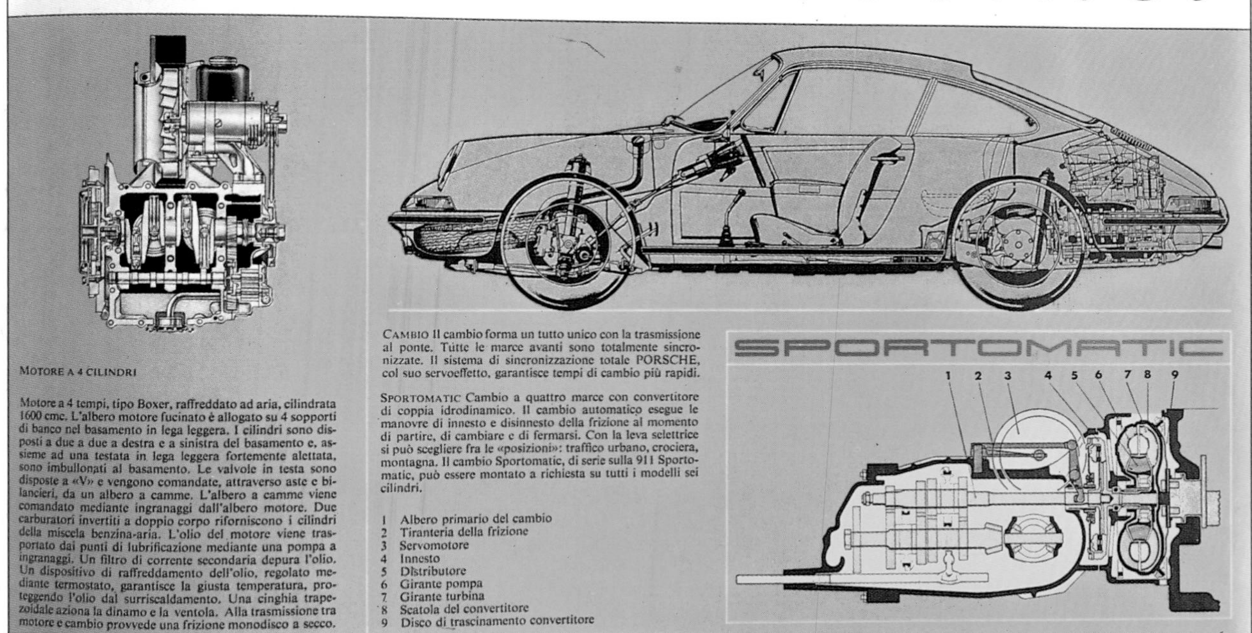

MOTORE A 4 CILINDRI

Motore a 4 tempi, tipo Boxer, raffreddato ad aria, cilindrata 1600 cmc. L'albero motore fucinato è allogato su 4 sopporti di banco nel basamento in lega leggera. I cilindri sono disposti a due a due a destra e a sinistra del basamento e, assieme ad una testata in lega leggera fortemente alettata, sono imbullonati al basamento. Le valvole in testa sono disposte a «V» e vengono comandate, attraverso aste e bilancieri, da un albero a camme. L'albero a camme viene comandato mediante ingranaggi dall'albero motore. Due carburatori invertiti a doppio corpo riforniscono i cilindri della miscela benzina-aria. L'olio del motore viene trasportato dai punti di lubrificazione mediante una pompa a ingranaggi. Un filtro di corrente secondaria depura l'olio. Un dispositivo di raffreddamento dell'olio, regolato mediante termostato, garantisce la giusta temperatura, proteggendo l'olio dal surriscaldamento. Una cinghia trapezoidale aziona la dinamo e la ventola. Alla trasmissione tra motore e cambio provvede una frizione monodisco a secco.

CAMBIO Il cambio forma un tutto unico con la trasmissione al ponte. Tutte le marce avanti sono totalmente sincronizzate. Il sistema di sincronizzazione totale PORSCHE, col suo servoeffetto, garantisce tempi di cambio più rapidi.

SPORTOMATIC Cambio a quattro marce con convertitore di coppia idrodinamico. Il cambio automatico esegue le manovre di innesto e disinnesto della frizione al momento di partire, di cambiare e di fermarsi. Con la leva selettrice si può scegliere fra le «posizioni»: traffico urbano, crociera, montagna. Il cambio Sportomatic, di serie sulla 911 Sportomatic, può essere montato a richiesta su tutti i modelli sei cilindri.

1 Albero primario del cambio
2 Tiranteria della frizione
3 Servomotore
4 Innesto
5 Distributore
6 Girante pompa
7 Girante turbina
8 Scatola del convertitore
9 Disco di trascinamento convertitore

LEFT, 1967–70: *The S models were only available with five-speed manual transmission, but the other two models offered this as an option to the standard four-speed unit along with a semi-automatic transmission known as the 'Sportmatic'. This was primarily designed for the US market and was basically an electro-hydraulic system which eliminated the clutch pedal, replacing it with a switch on the gear lever which operated a solenoid to disengage the single dry-plate clutch fitted between the torque convertor and gearbox.*

RIGHT, 1967: *Ventilated disc brakes were fitted on all four wheels, and Koni shock absorbers replaced the standard units. A rear anti-roll bar was also added. Externally, the most obvious distinguishing feature of the new 911S was the debut of the classic Fuchs five-spoke alloy wheels. The new model was well received by motoring journalists who praised the extra flexibility that the more powerful engine gave, whilst warning of the increased ability that it provided for inducing sudden oversteer at the limit of adhesion, which was still a problem, mainly because of the skinny tyres which were fitted.*

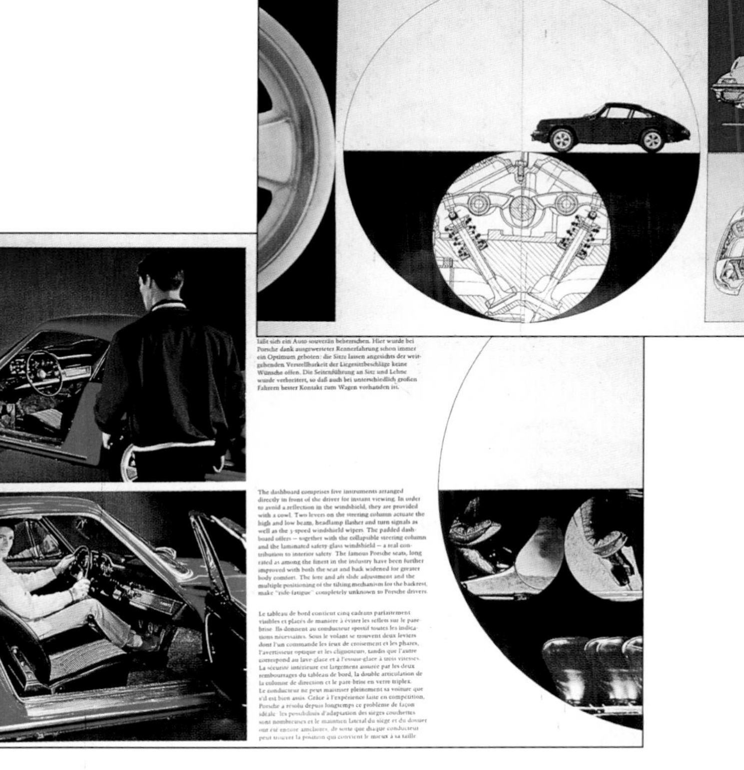

The dashboard comprises five instruments arranged directly in front of the driver for instant viewing. In order to avoid a reflection in the windshield, they are provided with a cowl. Two levers on the steering column actuate the high and low beam, headlamp flasher and turn signals as well as the 3-speed windshield wipers. The padded dashboard offers – together with the collapsible steering column and the laminated safety glass windshield – a real contribution to interior safety. The famous Porsche seats, long rated as among the finest in the industry have been further improved with both the seat and back widened for greater body comfort. The fore and aft slide adjustment and the multiple positioning of the tilting mechanism for the backrest, make "ride-fatigue" completely unknown to Porsche drivers.

Le tableau de bord contient cinq cadrans parfaitement visibles et placés de manière à éviter les reflets sur le pare-brise. Ils donnent au conducteur sportif toutes les indications nécessaires. Sous le volant se trouvent deux leviers dont l'un commande les feux de croisement et les phares, l'avertisseur optique et les clignoteurs, tandis que l'autre correspond au lave-glace et à l'essuie-glace à trois vitesses. La sécurité intérieure est largement assurée par les deux rembourrages du tableau de bord, la double articulation de la colonne de direction et le pare-brise en verre triplex. Le conducteur ne peut maîtriser pleinement sa voiture que s'il est bien assis. Grâce à l'expérience faite en compétition, ...

BELOW LEFT, 1968: *In 1968, the B-series 911 was introduced. This featured a wheelbase increased by 2.25 inches by extending the rear trailing arms. By changing the driveshaft design, the engine/transmission unit remained in its original position which improved the front/rear weight distribution. The track was widened slightly and the rear wheelarches mildly flared to accommodate this, allowing for wider wheel rims to be fitted to the higher-performance models. There were three models available, the 911T, 911E and 911S. The 'T' did not stand for Targa as is often mistakenly assumed. In fact the 911T was a 'base' model with 110bhp available, giving a top speed of 'only' 124mph (198kph). The E and S models were now fitted with fuel injection systems which raised their outputs to 140 and 170bhp respectively.*

COMFORT
SAFETY
PERFORMANCE

911E
911S

Porsche production models have always closely reflected the knowledge and experience gained in competition, and in the latest models this is true to an exceptional degree. In the Type 911 E and 911 S models, for example, fuel injection (used in Porsche competition cars for 3 years) is now standard. Brake horsepower developed shows a marked increase to 158 b.h.p. (SAE) for the 911 E and 190 b.h.p. (SAE) for the 911 S. Other advantages are improved torque at lower engine speeds, better fuel consumption figures and engine performance unaffected when driving at varying heights above sea level. These points all show to advantage in the 911 E which, perhaps, can best be described as the Porsche Grand Touring model "par excellence".

The "S" engine develops its increased power in the upper r.p.m. range, necessitating full use of the gearbox to obtain the maximum performance available. The stiffer suspension of the 911 S is in keeping with its high speeds on the open road, and its suitability for use in competition.

The 911 E, on the other hand, while retaining excellent allround handling qualities, because of the emphasis on maximum touring comfort, has a self-levelling hydro-pneumatic front suspension. In addition to the improvement obtained in ride comfort, this new suspension results in the ground clearance remaining constant, while as another point of interest, the angle of the headlamp beams does not vary when on rough roads.

Directional stability and neutral cornering characteristics of the 911 E and 911 S, together with the other models in the range, have been still further improved by an increase of 2¼" in the wheelbase, which results in a better front and rear weight distribution.

A further advantage resulting from the increased wheelbase is enhanced ride comfort over bad roads. To keep pace with the greater horsepower now available, the 911 E and 911 S models are fitted as standard with high-speed tyres and larger brake calipers are also fitted.

ABOVE, 1970: *1970 brought the first significant engine change with an increase in capacity to 2.2 litres. All three models, T, E and S, were retained with otherwise basically unchanged specifications.*

LEFT AND BELOW, 1970: *Externally the 2.2-litre cars differed little from the previous model other than for a discreet decal in the rear window designating the capacity change. Decals are not the most enduring marking system, so this will probably have disappeared from most of the remaining examples making it very difficult to distinguish them on the road.*

LEFT, 1970: *The major beneficial result of the engine capacity change was that the 911 was able to meet the more stringent US emission laws without having recourse to leaning-down the mixture settings of the engines, as did most other rival manufacturers. This meant that the cars ran smoother and on lower octane fuels.*

RIGHT, 1972: *A further engine size increase took place in 1972 with all models getting the new 2341cc unit. Externally these models were distinguished by the mildly-optimistic '2.4' badges on the right of the engine cover air intake grille.*

Auch Komfort ist für den Porsche kein Luxus.

Über all den Rennerfolgen vergißt man leicht, daß die Mehrheit aller Porsche im Alltagsverkehr gefahren werden. Weshalb sie auch in der großzügigen Ausstattung so komfortabel sind wie teure Reiselimousinen. Der Innenraum und die Armaturen sind streng funktionell gestaltet. Die Bedienungselemente sind schnell und mühelos zu erreichen. Alle Kontrollarmaturen liegen blendfrei im Blickfeld, so daß die wichtigen Betriebsdaten sofort ablesbar sind. Selbst der Ausfall eines der beiden Bremskreise wird von einer Kontrolleuchte angezeigt.

Fahrer und Beifahrer haben im Innenraum ungehinderte Bewegungsfreiheit. Die anatomisch richtig geformten Vordersitze liegen im Schwerpunkt des Wagens. Durch ihre Schalenform geben sie dem Fahrer Seitenhalt und machen ihm auch auf längeren Strecken das Fahren angenehm.

Der Porsche hat zwei Zusatzsitze. Klappt man ihre Lehnen herunter, so entsteht ein Gepäckraum mit ca. 235 l Inhalt. Er ist eine praktische Ergänzung zum vorderen Kofferraum, der durch die raumsparende Vorderachse 200 l abschließbaren Gepäckraum bietet. Voll ausgekleidet mit Nadelfilz, damit Ihr Gepäck nicht hin- und herrutscht und nicht an den Kanten beschädigt wird.

Bei allen Vorzügen ist der Porsche für viele Autofahrer nichts weiter als ein schicker Wagen, der auf der Autobahn alles hinter sich läßt. Mehr nicht. Daß der Porsche mehr ist – vielleicht eine automobiltechnische Welt für sich – läßt sich nur erkennen, wenn man ihn fährt. Z. B. zunächst einmal bei Ihrem Porschehändler zur Probe.

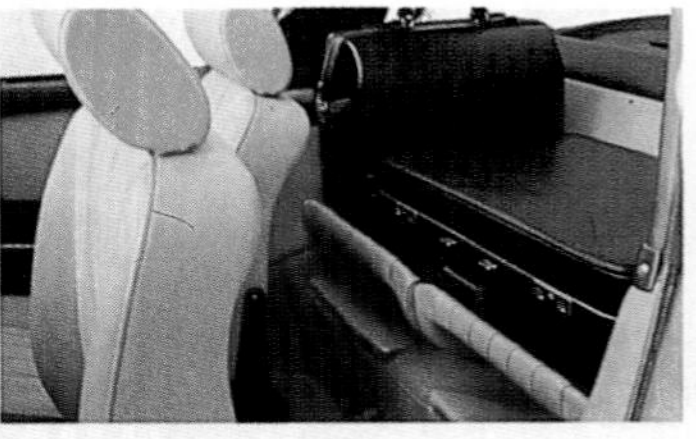

ABOVE, 1972: *The three model line-up was again retained, but all three were now fuel-injected. Output was correspondingly increased, with the top 911S variant now producing 190bhp. This resulted in a 0–60mph acceleration time of just 6 seconds and a top speed of 140mph (227kph) whilst comfortably meeting even the tough California emission standards. To help reduce front-end lift at high speed, the 911S was fitted with a chin spoiler under the front bumper. This was offered as an option on the other two models, but proved so popular that it was subsequently made standard on all of the cars.*

TOP RIGHT, 1972: *Another minor external change was the addition of an external filler point for the engine oil tank on the right rear wing just behind the door. This only lasted for a year owing to the inability of service station attendants to distinguish it from the fuel filler, with disastrous results.*

RIGHT, 1972: *Eminently functional, the interior had never received rave reviews, a description 'comfortably elegant' being about the top rating given by a tester. Then again, it has never been highly criticized either, which must mean that the compromise was about right.*

RIGHT, 1977: *1974 brought the first major redesign of the car. Several events combined to bring this about. Firstly increased US safety regulations, demanded bumpers capable of withstanding 5mph impacts undamaged, along with increased standards for resistance to side impacts. Also, further reductions in the exhaust emission standards were introduced and to add to this the Middle East War produced a stinging petrol price increase. Faced with all of this, most car manufacturers further detuned their engines or introduced bogus economy models and fitted them with ugly and heavy shock-absorbing bumpers. However, as we have seen, Porsche are not the same as most car manufacturers. Their answer was to introduce their most powerful models yet, which to most commentators appeared, in the circumstances, to be commercial suicide.*

LEFT, 1977: *There was, however, solid logic behind the move. The new cars were restyled to include the mandatory US market 5mph impact bumpers. The logic was that what the Americans demand today, others will demand tomorrow. So whereas most manufacturers produced costly add-ons for their US export models, Porsche reduced production costs by standardizing.*

BOTTOM LEFT, 1977: *To compensate for this, and the new US emission regulations, engine capacity once again increased, this time to 2.7 litres to match the Carrera introduced the previous year, featured on later pages. Two models were offered, the base 911 producing 143bhp and the new 911S 167bhp. The latter was nearer in specification to the old 911E, with the Carrera adopting the mantle of the 'Hot' version. Despite being some 12 per cent down on power, the 2.7 911S was faster than the 2.4-litre version, and once again more tractable thanks to the addition of the Bosch K-Jetronic fuel injection system. Inside the cars acquired new highback seats and over the next few years a lot of extra equipment was added to increase the creature comforts. By the time the 2.7-litre cars finished their production span, a vastly improved heater, two-speed wipers with intermittent setting, two-stage rear window heater and headlamp washers were all standard.*

"Faster" than the Engine: Porsche Suspension

From the earliest days, prompted by considerations of safety and a sense of responsibility, every Porsche model has been provided with a suspension which is "faster" than the engine.

In the 911 SC, independent front suspension is by radius arms and MacPherson struts; rear suspension is independent with alloy semi-trailing arms and transverse torsion bars.

Anti-roll bars – 20 mm in front and 18 mm at the back – minimise body roll and enhance the traction of the low profile tyres.

The Turbo's modified steering geometry, for front and rear axles, proves that a fast ride need not be a rough one. In this the ultra low profile 50-series tyres, specially developed for the Turbo, play a vital part. Their 50% aspect ratio (twice breadth to height) sets totally new safety standards in all conditions, i. e. at speed, cornering, braking and water dispersal.

Fitted to forged alloy rims – 7-inch wide in the front and 8-inch at the rear – they are housed under flared wheel arches. These tyres are also available for the 911 SC, though because of the narrower wheel arches, they are here fitted to 6-inch (front) and 7-inch (rear) rims.

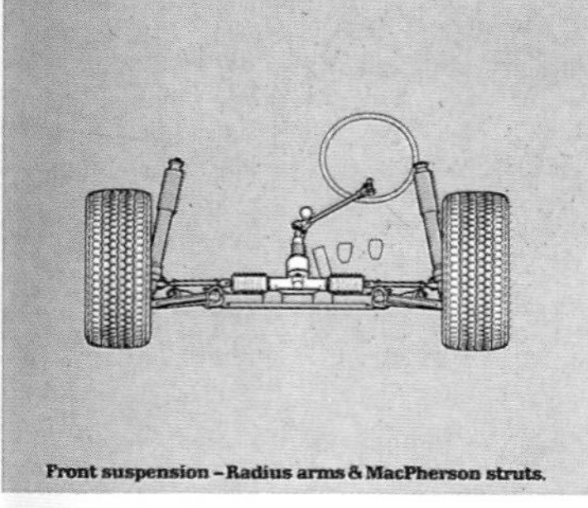

Front suspension – Radius arms & MacPherson struts.

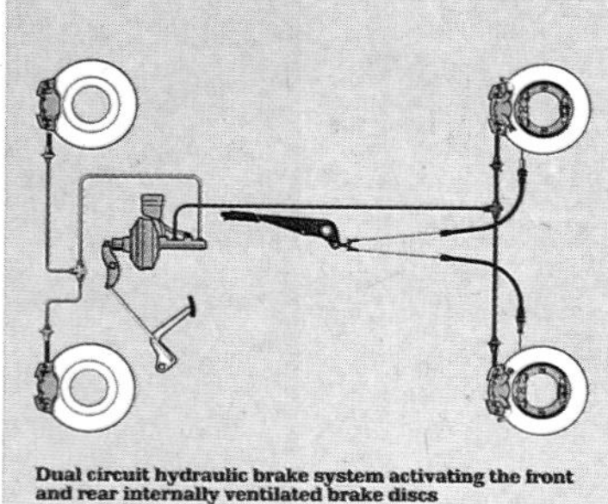

Dual circuit hydraulic brake system activating the front and rear internally ventilated brake discs

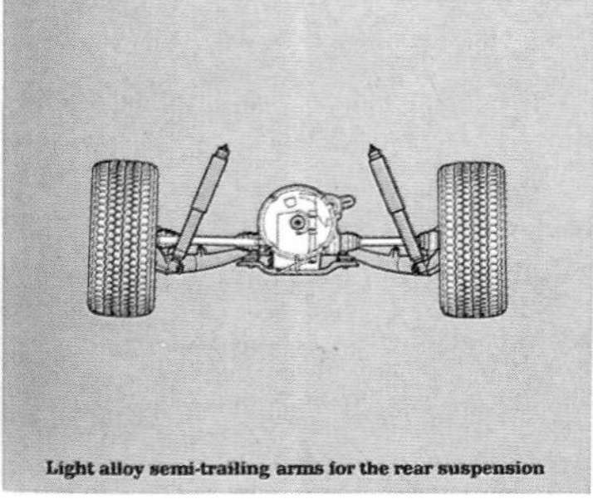

Light alloy semi-trailing arms for the rear suspension

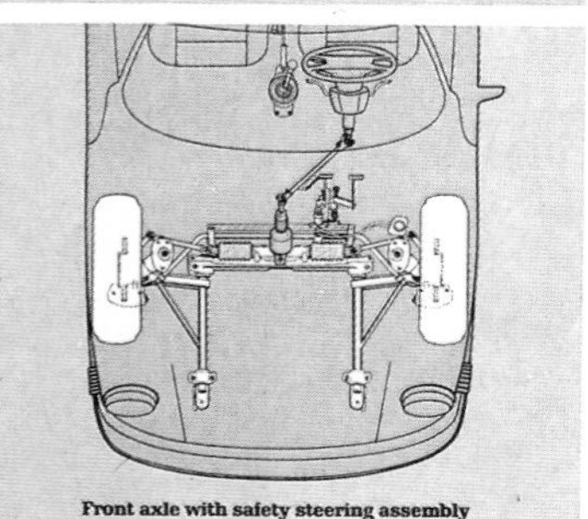

Front axle with safety steering assembly

ABOVE, 1981: *In 1978, only two 911 models would be offered. At the top of the list was the awesome Turbo, of which more later. The other model was the SC, literally a Carrera without the name. Engine capacity was now 3 litres developing 180bhp and generous amounts of torque across the range. The wheelarches were flared more heavily to accommodate the new, much wider, standard tyres. Electronic ignition was now also standard as was the US emission-required air pump. In 1980, electric windows and air conditioning became standard. 1981 brought halogen headlights, rear seatbelts and a seven-year anti-rust warranty.*

LEFT, 1983: *During the five-year life of the SC the mechanical specification changed little, but the equipment levels continued to improve as the cars became more sophisticated. In 1982, the sound system was uprated and heated door mirrors arrived. Then in 1983, a Cabriolet finally joined the line-up. This was the first factory-built soft-top model for nearly twenty years, and is covered in more detail on page 64.*

RIGHT, 1984: *The name Carrera returned for 1984 to mark another mechanical upgrade. Externally, the only obvious difference from the previous SC models were the twin foglights incorporated into the front spoiler beneath the bumper. Under the skin a further enlargement of the engine to 3.2 litres and the addition of Bosch 'Motronic' fuel injection increased power output to 200bhp. A corresponding increase in torque brought greater flexibility and improved fuel economy. In 1985, power-adjusted front seats were included in the specification (as an option) and central-locking also became available, again as an option.*

THE PASSIVE SAFETY OF THE STEERING SYSTEM

In the 911, the steering gear and steering wheel mounting column lie in different planes, connected by an intermediate shaft with universal joints at both ends. In an accident, the intermediate shaft ensures that the steering system will yield through lateral or rotary deflection, while a heavy-duty mounting bracket provides an additional deformation path to prevent any hazardous displacement of the steering wheel into the vehicle interior. Steering wheel displacement was measured in crash tests at about 50km/h against a fixed barrier. Here the results showed that horizontal steering wheel displacement in the Porsche 911 fell below the legally permitted maximum of 127 mm by a considerable margin.

A dummy is used to determine impact forces on the steering wheel in every position to which it can be adjusted. Here a whole series of measures plays an important part in keeping impact forces and the risk of injury in the Porsche 911 to a minimum.

The yielding crash pad is shatterproof and well-padded. By converting kinetic energy into programmed deformation activity, the load it would apply in a collision is rendered much less hazardous to the driver.

The steering shaft mounting is designed to yield on impact, thus creating an important deformation path. A further deformation element is situated immediately under the crash pad. In the first phase of the collision it aligns the steering wheel in the direction of the impact forces, thereby dispersing them over the largest possible area of the crash pad and reducing their effect at individual points of impact.

In all matters relating to safety all Porsche 911 models are exceptional vehicles, incorporating design features for both passive and active safety and a degree of attention to personal comfort and protection entirely in keeping with their high performance, while being engineered to comply with safety standards to an extent far beyond those generally applied to motor vehicles today.

RIGHT, 1986: *A 'Turbo-look' package was also offered as an option. This effectively consisted of the Turbo's body/chassis combined with Carrera running gear for a premium of around 30 per cent extra on top of the normal Carrera price.*

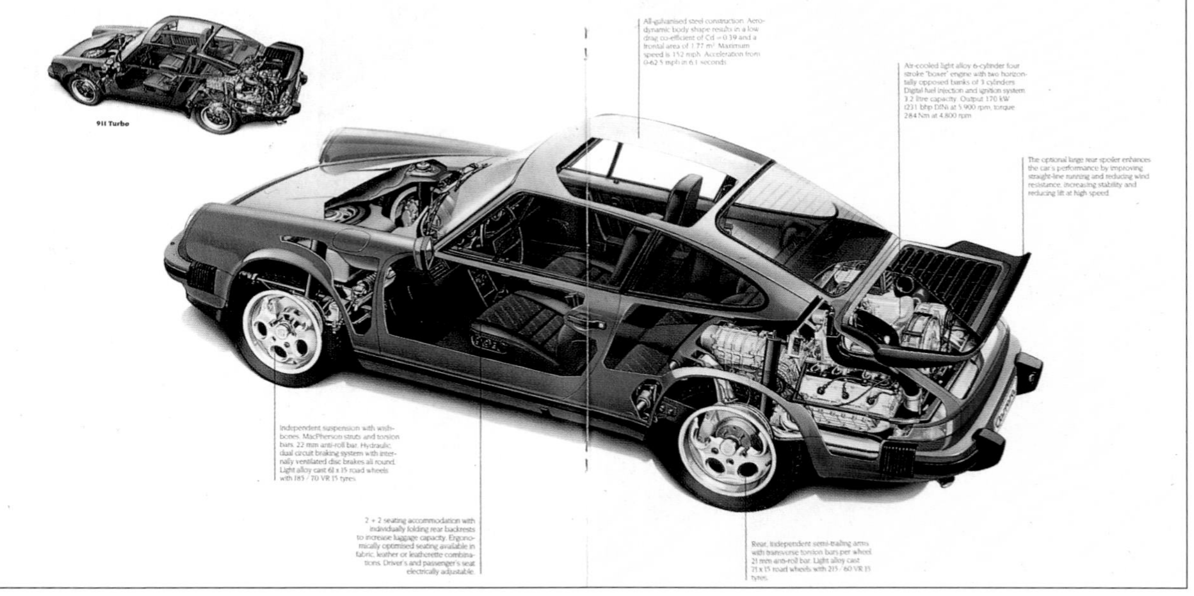

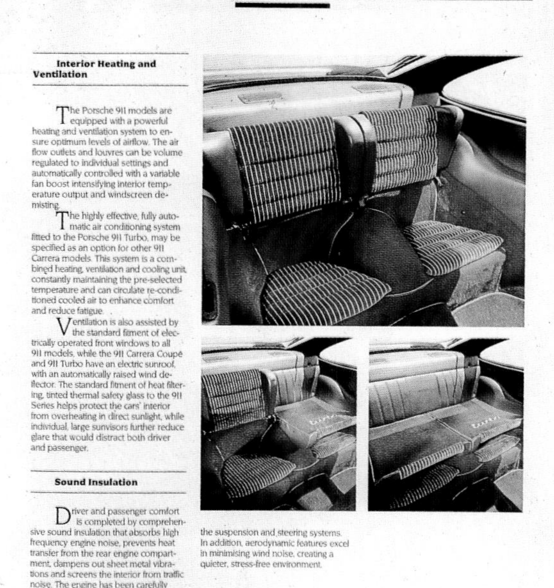

Interior Safety and Comfort

Interior Heating and Ventilation

The Porsche 911 models are equipped with a powerful heating and ventilation system to ensure optimum levels of airflow. The air flow outlets and louvres can be volume regulated to individual settings and automatically controlled with a variable fan boost intensifying interior temperature output and windscreen demisting.

The highly effective, fully automatic air conditioning system fitted to the Porsche 911 Turbo, may be specified as an option for other 911 Carrera models. This system is a combined heating, ventilation and cooling unit, constantly maintaining the pre-selected temperature and can circulate re-conditioned cooled air to enhance comfort and reduce fatigue.

Ventilation is also assisted by the standard fitment of electrically operated front windows to all 911 models, while the 911 Carrera Coupé and 911 Turbo have an electric sunroof, with an automatically raised wind deflector. The standard fitment of heat filtering, tinted thermal safety glass to the 911 Series helps protect the cars' interior from overheating in direct sunlight, while individual, large sunvisors further reduce glare that would distract both driver and passenger.

Sound Insulation

Driver and passenger comfort is completed by comprehensive sound insulation that absorbs high frequency engine noise, prevents heat transfer from the rear engine compartment, dampens out sheet metal vibrations and screens the interior from traffic noise. The engine has been carefully dampened against vibration, as have the suspension and steering systems. In addition, aerodynamic features excel in minimising wind noise, creating a quieter, stress-free environment.

LEFT, 1986: *Only minor amendments took place in 1986, mainly to the air conditioner and gear change linkage. Front seats were lowered slightly to give additional headroom and a new heavier-duty windscreen washing system was added. For 1987, more power was added to the engine, up from 200 to 214bhp. This was mainly brought about by recalibration work on the electronic injection system, which also raised torque by a further 5 per cent. A new five-speed gearbox was introduced with cone-type synchromesh, and clutch operation changed from mechanical to a hydraulic system. 1988 would be the final year for this model prior to the next major design. The only changes were the adoption of certain options, such as central locking and cruise control as standard. After 25 years, the 911 had evolved considerably, yet retained its original character. It was easier to drive, but still demanded full attention of the driver. In a world of boring clones, an individual still survived.*

ABOVE, 1990: *The word radical has never featured much in the vocabulary of Porsche engineers, more in the text of the road testers. However, in the case of the Carrera 2, introduced in 1988, the word must have appeared somewhere in the design brief, because this 'new' 911 contains only 17 per cent of parts which are interchangeable with the previous Carrera models. Neither was it coincidental that this model was unveiled in the year which marked the 911's 25th anniversary.*

ABOVE, 1990: *Although it retains its classic 'boxer' 6-cylinder layout, the 3.6-litre engine is virtually a new unit. It features twin ignition systems combined with a Bosch Motronic engine management system, revised inlet manifolds and a new exhaust system, to produce 250bhp even when fitted with a catalytic convertor and running on unleaded fuel. The engine has been partially encapsulated to reduce noise emissions. A new five-speed gearbox is fitted, as well as power steering, and an ABS braking system.*

LEFT AND BELOW, 1990: *The silhouette of the Carrera 2 more closely resembles the first 911 than it does its immediate predecessor. The lines are much cleaner with none of the add-ons which the car had sprouted over the years. Aerodynamics have thus been greatly improved and the cd value lowered from 0.395 to 0.32. The rear spoiler automatically extends from its housing on the engine cover at 50mph (80kph), and retracts below 6mph (9.6kph).*

PORSCHE 911: A CLASSIC AHEAD OF ITS TIME

The Porsche 911 is the epitome of engineering excellence. Continuing to carry the evocative "Carrera" designation, both the 911 Carrera 2 and 911 Carrera 4 set new standards in high performance motoring.

Although over 85% of the components of the Carrera 2 and 4 are new, the redesigned, aerodynamically optimised bodystyle remains faithful to the classic lines of the original 911 design.

Numerous subtle but significant changes to the body by the engineers at the Development Centre at Weissach have produced a design of classic elegance and impressive aerodynamic efficiency.

Advanced new polyurethane front and rear body panels are both in keeping with the car's sleek contours and help to optimise the airflow over the car.

Deformable to minimise damage to the bodywork in a light impact, these panels encase resilient shock absorbing bumpers.

The new 911 Carreras are also the first full production Porsches to inherit the smooth underbody floor panels developed from the Le Mans winning Porsche 956 and 962. These underbody panels optimise the airflow under the car, at the same time as reducing lift through the benefits of ground effect technology.

Together with the more aerodynamic bonded windscreen, smooth rain gutters and the streamlined sill mouldings, these aerodynamic improvements combine to significantly reduce the drag-coefficient to 0.32, exceptionally low within this high performance class.

Another major benefit of this advanced new body design is the reduction of destabilising lift to near zero, greatly improving roadholding at high speed.

To maintain this optimum airflow at speed, there is a unique retractable rear aerodynamic spoiler.

Automatically extending at around 50 mph, this advanced spoiler both increases downforce and doubles the volume of engine air-intake for more efficient cooling. To maintain the purity of the classic 911 body design, the spoiler retracts at around 6 mph.

The aerodynamic improvements of the new 911 Series are tuned to a highly advanced chassis and driveline. With a choice of two-wheel or all-wheel-drive systems, the 911 Carrera is equipped with the latest development of the legendary flat six engine, now producing an impressive 250 bhp.

It is no wonder then that the new 911 Series represents one of the most powerful yet composed high performance cars in the world. And now equipped with anti-lock brakes and available with a controlled 3-way catalytic converter, both driver and environmental safety can be assured.

Integral foglamps and indicators are recessed to improve aerodynamics

Aerodynamic refinements to the new 911 Carrera include front and rear deformable polyurethane body panels to help optimise the airflow.

The deformable body panels encase resilient shock absorbing bumpers.

The powerful headlights are kept clean with a high pressure water jet.

ABOVE, 1990: *One of the very few options currently offered on the Carrera 2 is the new Tiptronic Gearbox. This is a computer-controlled automatic transmission which gives the driver the choice between conventional automatic gear selection, or clutchless manual selection. In manual mode, the computer monitors the driving style being used and chooses one of five gear selection programmes to provide gear changes matched to the driver's requirements. Gimmicky? Maybe, but one thing is certain, the Carrera 2 provides style and performance which not only matches its era, but gives the basis for a further 25 years of development.*

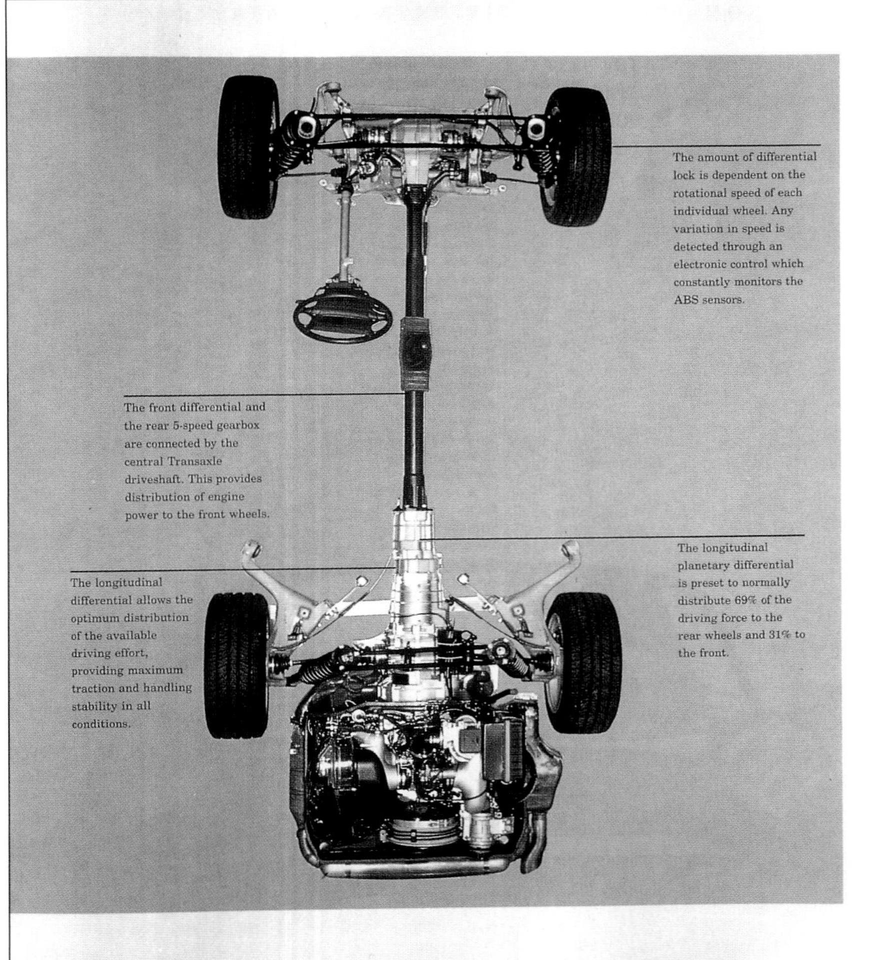

BELOW, 1990: *Torque is normally split 31 per cent front to 69 per cent rear, but distribution can be varied through locking devices on the central differential unit which allow more drive to be transmitted to the axle most capable of handling it. Consequently the system automatically adjusts to the driving conditions. A computer constantly monitors wheel speeds and controls the various locking devices.*

The 911 Carrera 4 is the first full production car in the world to utilise an 'intelligent' all-wheel-drive system. This technology is the culmination of over eight years of development combined with the experience gained from testing the system both on the road and in arduous competition.

The dynamic all-wheel-drive system of the 911 Carrera 4 represents the very latest development of this technology.

Building on the experience gained with the Porsche 959, it allows the driver to exploit the Carrera 4's power and handling to the full.

A new central driveshaft tube leads from the 5-speed gearbox at the rear of the car to the front axle. This allows the distribution of engine power to the front wheels using an advanced longitudinal differential with hydraulic control.

Whilst under extreme conditions 100% of the available driving power can be delivered solely to the front or rear wheels, this unique planetary differential is preset to normally distribute 69% of the driving force to the rear wheels and 31% to the front.

This retains the classic rear-wheel drive character of the 911 Carrera and allows both optimum traction and handling stability in all conditions.

However, should any of the wheels begin to spin due to loss of traction, this will be recognised using individual electronic sensors. Driving traction will be maintained by the progressive operation of hydraulically operated locks in the longitudinal differential that engage to re-distribute the available driving effort.

This is achieved using an electronic control unit which constantly compares the rotational speed of each individual wheel using the ABS sensors. If the microprocessor detects a difference in speed between the wheels of even as small as 0.5 mph, the hydraulically controlled longitudinal differential will engage, a process taking only 25 milliseconds. So advanced is this system that it can even detect and correct for any variation in wheel rotational speeds caused by differing tyre pressures.

A further innovation of the all-wheel-drive system is the inclusion of an electronically controlled transverse differential, its function being two-fold.

Firstly, it counteracts oversteer by producing an optimum distribution of the available driving effort between the rear wheels. Secondly, a manually controlled 'Traction Programme' allows maximum low-speed traction in the most adverse conditions by locking both the transverse and longitudinal differentials.

The 911 Carrera 4 truly represents a new era for the driving legend.

The 911 Carrera 4 combines high performance with supreme driving safety.

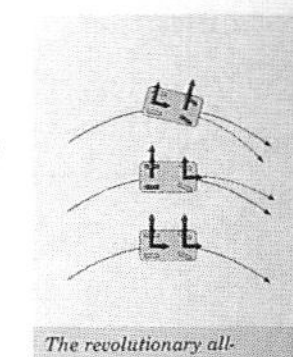
The revolutionary all-wheel-drive system is the most advanced in the world.

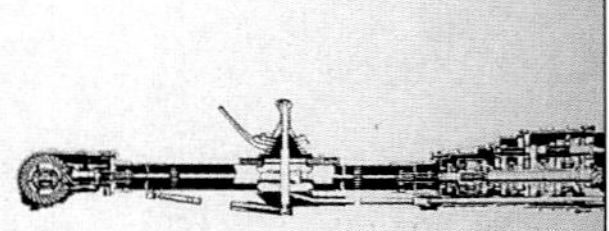
The longitudinal planetary differential electronically distributes the driving force between all four wheels of the 911 Carrera 4.

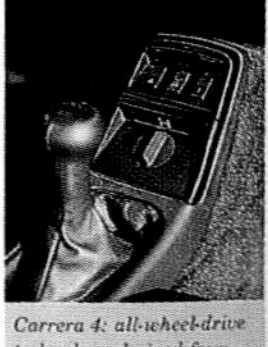
Carrera 4: all-wheel-drive technology derived from the Porsche 959.

ABOVE, 1990: *In 1988, alongside the new models the Carrera 4 was announced, featuring all the features of the Carrera 2 plus four-wheel drive. The new transmission design was based upon experience gained from the dynamic control system of the 959, which is featured in Chapter 11. Drive is provided to the front wheels via a driveshaft taken from the front of the gearbox and housed in a tube similar to that used on the 944 series.*

ABOVE, 1990: *The Carrera 4 is probably the ultimate development of the 911 line, at least for the present. It features a normally-aspirated engine producing power and torque only 12.5 per cent lower than the most powerful 911 Turbo engine, yet runs on unleaded fuel. It will reach 60mph in under 6 seconds, and has a top speed of over 160mph (260kph). The aerodynamic body produces zero lift and the suspension/ transmission package gives handling which is totally neutral. This, then, is Porsche's Supercar for the 1990s and beyond . . .*

RIGHT, 1982: *Although the Targa variant of the 911 had been in production virtually since the inception of the car, it was never considered to be a true 'open' model, primarily because of the fixed roll-over bar and glazed rear window. So, under the direction of the then new company chairman, Peter Schutz, a true convertible was introduced in 1982. This model was called the Cabriolet, and was the first factory-produced soft-top Porsche since the demise of the 356 nearly 20 years earlier, and even stronger links with tradition were maintained by the body production being carried out by the Reutter Division of the company. With the hood down and windows raised, the convertible was free of the customary buffeting generated at speed, mainly due to the superior aerodynamics of the 911 compared with its predecessor. Nevertheless top speed was reduced by some 10 per cent because of the added drag compared with the normal coupe.*

LEFT, 1982: *The hood was manual in operation and relatively easy to use. Spring-loaded concealed steel cables and panels helped not only with the operation, but also kept the hood taught at high speed when closed. When folded, a neat cover kept everything tidy, and the compact design allowed for the unmodified retention of the rear seats. The rear window was a plastic zip-out panel.*

LEFT, 1987: *The Cabriolet body has subsequently been offered on Turbo variants as well as the Carreras, and body options were also available, one of which was the Flat Nose. This was a design which gave a much more streamlined front-end shape, with pop-up headlights and louvred wing panels. It had been initially developed for the 935 racing models, but so many aftermarket 'rip-off' kits had appeared that Porsche decided to offer the option themselves through their new 'Sonderwünsch' division, which offered custom-built options.*

ABOVE, 1991: *These options were not cheap, however, the Flat Nose adding some 30 per cent to the price of a new Turbo Cabriolet, and if combined with the Turbo-look kit it would double the price of a Carrera.*

BELOW, 1989: *The windscreen is lower, reshaped and more steeply raked. A simpler hood is also fitted. In the lowered position, it is covered by a moulded plastic cover. No side quarter windows are fitted, and electric windows and central locking are also omitted. However, in deference to modern tastes, the air conditioning, hi-fi system, motorized leather-upholstered seats and electric mirrors are retained in the standard specification.*

RIGHT, 1989: *All of this makes the Speedster somewhat of an anachronism to both potential buying groups, being too impractical for medallion-man and not 'basic' enough for the hair-shirt enthusiast. Regardless, it is probably the best 911 posermobile yet, and as such will guarantee the continual escalation in value of the few examples that will have been made. In 20 years' time, this is the Porsche 911 which will be changing hands at auction for Fine Art prices alongside Bugattis, Ferraris and the like.*

ABOVE, 1989: *Another revival occurred in 1989 when the famous Speedster name briefly returned to the market. Thirty five years on from Max Hoffman's original conception of the 356 Speedster, there was still demand, particularly in America, for a cut-down open Porsche. So the same principles were applied to a 911 Cabriolet as had been all that time ago, and the result was the 911 Speedster.*

S-JS 9442

With the Touring car on the racetrack- in the Porsche Carrera RS

At the start: a new PORSCHE — the CARRERA RS.

The name reminds one of the longest and hardest road race in the world, in which Hans Herrmann, Fürst Metternich and José Herrarte once celebrated their triumphs in PORSCHE: The CARRERA PANAMERICANA.

The car's technique points out, in every detail, the sum of all the experience which PORSCHE has collected up until now, in sports and in this series of car.

Its performances will make a hard competitor out of him in the group 3 and 4.

The prominent rear spoiler, from which the car is instantly recognisable, improves the aerodynamics of the car and stabilize the road-grip.

The interior is designed for the sporting stakes. It escapes superbly from the superfluous and consists only of the functional necessities. Result: A power to weight ratio of 4.6 kg /HP.

Its speciality: It has none. Like an all-round competition vehicle, it is qualified in the same way for Slalom, track, mountain and Rally racing.

Its particularity: The CARRERA RS is without any restrictions, being fully practical for everyday traffic and roads. A purely simple PORSCHE, which can perform wholly unusual things.

Green light for a new PORSCHE: The CARRERA RS.

The motor is a 6-cylinder-inject-Cylinders opposed. 2687 ccm. 210 DIN-HP of 6300 r.p.m. Maximum torque 26 kpm.

Its test series produced a fantastic result regarding the drive performance: from 0 to 100 in 5.8 seconds. Top speed is 245 km /h. Nevertheless, it maintains a surprising elasticity for a maximum output motor over the whole number of corresponding r.p.m. sphere, with the highest efficiency between 3,000 and 5,000 r.p.m. With a compression of only 8.5:1, the CARRERA RS is satisfied even with standard petrol.

The power of the car makes the driver superior in every situation, and obliges him, at the same time, to give a good example to others in road traffic and on the race track.

Its repertoire: With axis to the race and back home. Monday to the office. Tuesday to Geneva. Back in the evening. Wednesday shopping. City. Traffic-jam. Crawling traffic, but no spark plug soot. Thursday high-road, Motorway, bends, field-paths, building plots. Friday only short distances and cold starts again. Saturday to Finland with the holiday luggage.

CARRERA RS — On the sprint as well as in the Marathon, it has fully inexhaustible reserves.

With the racing car in the town - in the Porsche Carrera RS

ABOVE, 1973: *The Carrera RS was the first of the special 911 models which were built primarily as customer racers, the RS standing for 'Rennsport' (Racing Sport). The Carrera RS was based on a 911S bodyshell which was lightened in every possible way. It had thinner sheet metal, thinner window glass and a fibre glass engine cover incorporating the unique duck-tail spoiler. The interior was stripped of all non-essential equipment, the rear seats were removed and the front ones were thinly padded bucket shells. Even the interior door handles were replaced by pull-cords.*

RIGHT, 1973: *All of this reduced the kerb weight by over 300lb (135kg). On top of all of this, the RS received the new 2.7-litre engine a year ahead of the production cars, giving 210bhp. Initially, 500 of these cars were to be built, but eventually over 1,600 left the factory, 600 of which were trimmed internally to standard 'S' specification and sold as road cars. Externally, all cars were white with large 'Carrera' scripts along the bottom of the doors on each side and matching coloured wheel centres.*

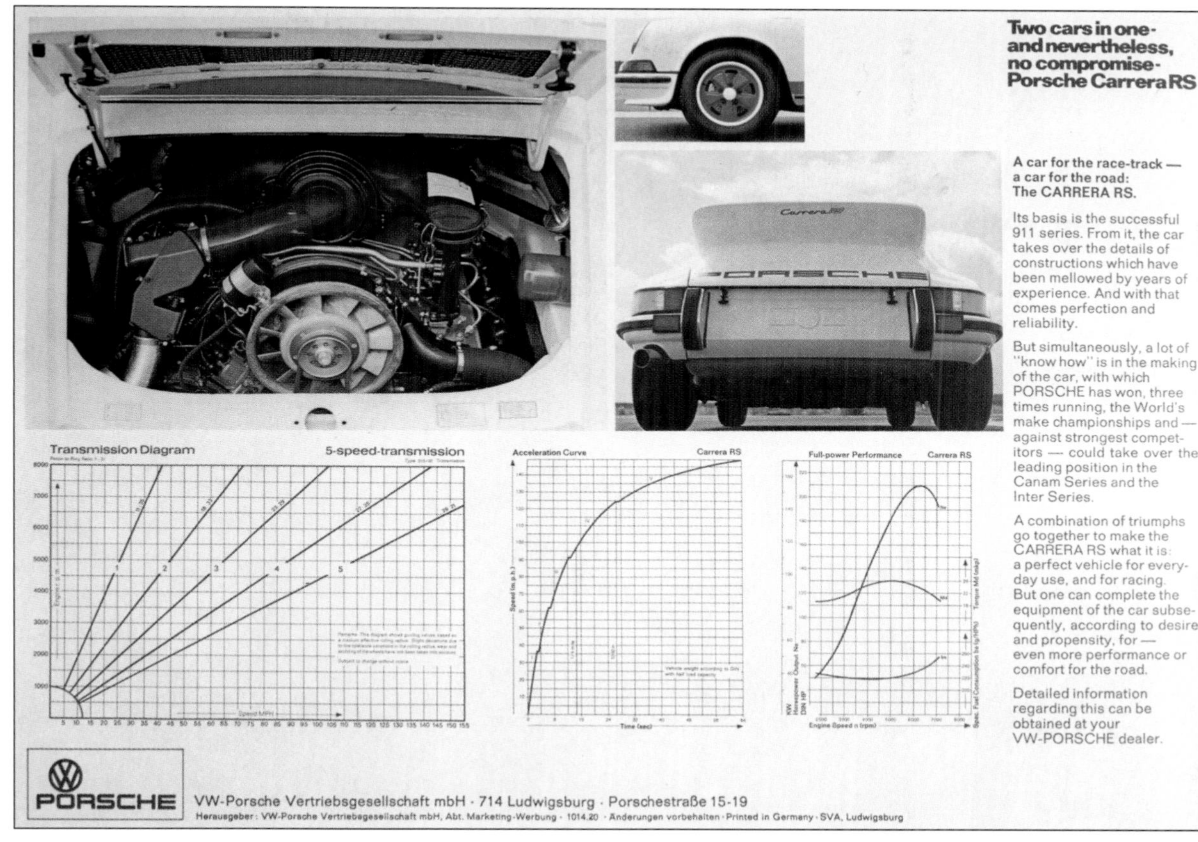

ABOVE, 1973: *Further modifications produced out-and-out racing variants such as the RSR with a 2.8-litre engine developing 300bhp. RS and RSR engine capacities were increased to 3 litres in 1974, raising outputs to 230 and 330bhp respectively. This car dominated Group 4 racing until the works began to devote more development time to the Turbo Carreras during 1976.*

ABOVE, 1975/76: *In 1972 Porsche was floated on the stock market as a public company for the first time. Ernst Fuhrmann, creator of the original quad-cam Carrera engine, became Chairman and, not surprisingly, brought engine development to the fore. Porsche had gained considerable experience of turbocharging through the 917 project and in 1974 had experimented at Le Mans with a turbocharged Carrera RSR with modified bodywork which earned it the undignified nickname of 'the Breadvan'.*

ABOVE, 1975/76: *By 1975, this development work had produced a new production model. Christened internally the 930, by the time it reached the market place it was renamed the Porsche Turbo.*

RIGHT, 1976: *The 930 featured a standard 3-litre engine fitted with a KKK turbocharger to produce 260bhp at 5500rpm. This, together with armfuls of torque, gave a 0–60mph time of under 5 seconds and a top speed of 156mph (252kph). The basic Turbo specification included air conditioning, electric windows, tinted glass and leather upholstery and was only available as a coupe.*

PORSCHE Turbo

It did not matter in which race the 1000 bhp, 12 cylinder 917/10s, or 917/30s, started, it was still no surprise who won - the Porsche Turbo. We could not gain any more experience by taking part in or winning more races, so the logical step was taken to put the immense know ledge gained into a production road-going car. This car is to be regarded as not only the flag-ship of our sales programme, but the crowning achievement of the 911 range. A milestone has been reached in the Porsche story, even though history already shows many instances where Porsche has shown other car manufacturers new methods and new technology. Now, turbo-charging. To pressurise the induction air, an energy source is utilised which otherwise just goes to waste - the exhaust gases.

This re-utilisation of the burnt fuel energy brings about an enormous increase in power even though compression ratios and engine speeds are lowered, noise is reduced and the exhaust gases become cleaner.

The Porsche Turbo is a unique blend of racing car efficiency, standards of interior equipment - previously only found in large luxurious saloons - and the docility of an everyday shopping car.

Such a blending of engineering sophistication leaves little to be desired by even the most fastidious driver or his fortunate passenger!

In every respect the Turbo is a new superlative due to the inbuilt experience which Porsche has gained from years of racing and production. Even though the Turbo reaches rarified heights, with its combination of exclusivity and aesthetic appeal, it is still a pure Porsche: robust, untemperamental, reliable, roadholding that makes the best of each driving condition - be it dry, rain or snow; untroubled by town driving, but most at home on the open road.

The Achilles heel of most high performance cars - everyday usage - is the Turbo's strong point. Yet another first - a star with an unlimited horizon - the Porsche Turbo.

The first drive in a Turbo is a fascinating experience - even for those who feel at home in fast or super fast cars - as even with a top speed in excess of 155 mph, It is the breathtaking acceleration which at 3,000 rpm changes the feel from gentle pressure in one's back to more of a push. Coupled with this feel, the engine whispers, while the chassis proves that harshness is not an essential element of speed. The ultra low profile tyres (width to height ratio of 2:1) provide a previously unknown standard of comfort in relation to their cornering powers. With 260 bhp behind, special engraved name plates in front, Turbo owners relax in seats of leather with genuine Scottish tartan inserts, while enjoying the stereo. Because, of course, the car is fitted with a self-seeking stereo radio with 4 loud-speakers, and an electrically operated aerial. The tinted glass all-round helps to maintain a pleasant temperature in summer, while in winter interior temperature is maintained by the thermostatically-controlled heating system. Visibility is looked after by the heated front windscreen, two-stage heating of the rear window, the headlamp washer system, rear window wiper, intermittent wipe setting, foglamps and the electrically operated windows.

LEFT, 1976: *The US export model, known as the Turbo Carrera, had a mildly detuned (245bhp) engine to cover the emission regulations, but even so, performance was barely altered. The suspension settings were beefed-up all around to match the extra power, and wider wheels and tyres were fitted. This did reduce the quality of the ride compared to the 'normal' 911 models, and the steering was heavier, but there were no complaints by owners who were getting the fastest 911 yet, with handling to match. In fact, one road tester branded the 930 as '. . . the finest blend of ultimate performance and refinement I have ever encountered . . .'*

Porsche 911 Turbo: Road Version of a World Champion

The 911 Turbo represents the acme of modern high-performance motoring. Being a direct descendant of the renowned Porsche 935, the car with several World Championships under its belt, the Turbo offers the ideal combination of civilized racebred road behaviour in everday motoring and sheer driving comfort.

As in the racing cars, the inlet air, after being boosted in the Turbo by the exhaust, is then cooled, thus permitting an even more efficient filling of the combustion chambers. The result: an astonishing 221 kW (300 bhp) from a mere 3.3 litre engine, which makes the 911 Turbo probably the fastest sports car up to 200 km/h with a top speed in excess of 260 km/h.

At such speeds the aerodynamic qualities of the Turbo's body become of fundamental importance. The front spoiler and – beyond the air intake for the intercooler – the large rear engine lid with its raised trailing edge reduce lift by nearly 100%, with consequent benefit to straight-line running, braking and cornering performance and steering, as well as directional stability in cross-winds.

LEFT, 1981: *Turbo specifications remained little changed until 1978 when, to coincide with the introduction of the SC, the Turbo's engine capacity was increased to 3.3 litres. This, together with the addition of an intercooler, raised output to 280bhp and torque to a whacking 303lb/ft. Even so, performance was barely changed as most of the changes ensured that the car met the ever-reducing exhaust emission limits around the world.*

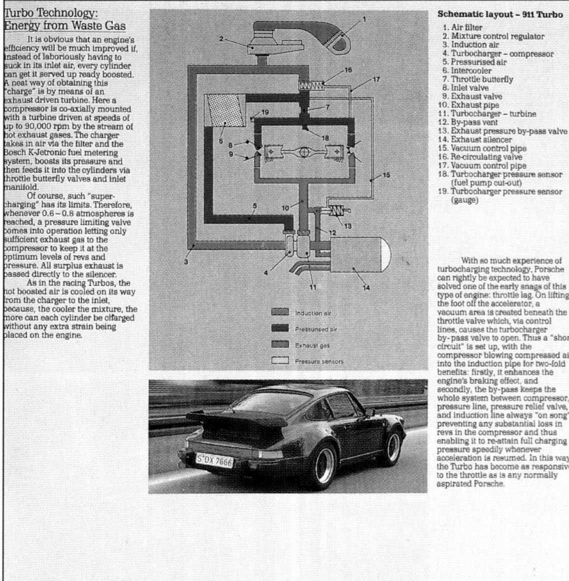

Turbo Technology: Energy from Waste Gas

It is obvious that an engine's efficiency will be much improved if, instead of laboriously having to suck in its inlet air, every cylinder can get it served up ready boosted. A neat way of obtaining this "charge" is by means of an exhaust driven turbine. Here a compressor is co-axially mounted with a turbine driven at speeds of up to 90,000 rpm by the stream of hot exhaust gases. The charger takes in air via the filter and the Bosch K-Jetronic fuel metering system, boosts its pressure and then feeds it into the cylinders via throttle butterfly valves and inlet manifold.

Of course, such "super-charging" has its limits. Therefore, whenever 0.6 – 0.8 atmospheres is reached, a pressure limiting valve comes into operation letting only sufficient exhaust gas to the compressor to keep it at the optimum levels of revs and pressure. All surplus exhaust is passed directly to the silencer.

As in the racing Turbos, the hot boosted air is cooled on its way from the charger to the inlet, because, the cooler the mixture, the more can each cylinder be charged without any extra strain being placed on the engine.

Schematic layout – 911 Turbo

1. Air filter
2. Mixture control regulator
3. Induction air
4. Turbocharger – compressor
5. Pressurised air
6. Intercooler
7. Throttle butterfly
8. Inlet valve
9. Exhaust valve
10. Exhaust pipe
11. Turbocharger – turbine
12. By-pass vent
13. Exhaust pressure by-pass valve
14. Exhaust silencer
15. Vacuum control pipe
16. Re-circulating valve
17. Vacuum control pipe
18. Turbocharger pressure sensor (fuel pump cut-out)
19. Turbocharger pressure sensor (gauge)

With so much experience of turbocharging technology, Porsche can rightly be expected to have solved one of the early snags of this type of engine: throttle lag. On lifting the foot off the accelerator, a vacuum area is created beneath the throttle valve which, via control lines, causes the turbocharger by-pass valve to open. Thus a "short circuit" is set up, with the compressor blowing compressed air into the induction pipe for two-fold benefits: firstly, it enhances the engine's braking effect, and secondly, the by-pass keeps the whole system between compressor, pressure line, pressure relief valve, and induction line always "on song", preventing any substantial loss in revs in the compressor and thus enabling it to re-attain full charging pressure speedily whenever acceleration is resumed. In this way the Turbo has become as responsive to the throttle as is any normally aspirated Porsche.

LEFT, 1981: *Further improvements were made to the suspension, and wheel diameter was increased to 16 inches (40cm) to allow fitment of lower profile tyres. Larger drilled brake discs were also fitted, with four piston callipers, originally used on the 917 race cars. The Turbo was dropped from the US market in 1979 in deference to energy resource concerns, but continued availability elsewhere led to increased 'black market' prices and brought its official return in 1986.*

LEFT, 1983: *The main differences were a 10 per cent increase in power, and 9-inch (22.5cm) wide wheels, bringing still more flaring to the wheelarches. This would be the final specification for the Turbo until it was dropped in 1989 to make way for the Carrera 2 & 4.*

ABOVE, 1983: *This absence did not last for long, however, because shortly before this book went to press, Porsche announced a new Turbo based on the Carrera 2 bodyshell and complete with all the trimmings, including the huge flared wheelarches and fixed rear spoiler which also accommodates the intercooler. 959-style 5-spoke alloy wheels are fitted, 17 inches (42.5cm) in diameter, to accommodate ultra-low profile tyres.*

RIGHT, 1986: *The 3.3-litre engine is retained, but revisions to the ignition, injection and exhaust systems plus larger turbocharger and intercooler raise power output still further to 320bhp, giving 0–60mph acceleration time of 4.8 seconds and a top speed of 168mph (272kph).*

ABOVE, 1987: *This was the quickest-ever 911 until a new limited-edition lightweight Carrera RS was introduced in 1991. The legend continues . . .*

912

When the new 911 was first put on sale in 1964, its price was almost 30 per cent higher than the most expensive 356 models, which were about to be phased-out. The quickest solution was to introduce an intermediate model to bridge the gap, and this was achieved by fitting the old 1600cc push-rod, four-cylinder engine into the new bodyshell. Thus the 912 was born.

The engine of the new 912 was slightly detuned to 90bhp, however, because of the more efficient aerodynamics of the new body, top speed was a more impressive 116mph (188kph), a slight improvement on the 356SC. A 12-volt electrical system was fitted, and a choice of four- or five-speed gearboxes was available.

Over the years, many attempts have been made by Porsche to introduce a cheap, entry-level model. These have almost always been frustrated not by lack of demand, but by the company's ability to sell more of its highly-priced, and therefore more profitable models, causing production to be switched away from the cheaper cars. One example of this was the 912.

cars. One example of this was the 912.

Although the 912 had a somewhat more austere look to the interior than the 911, the level of equipment was similar with reclining seats, three-speed wipers, reversing light and heated rear window all included in the standard specification. The introduction price was 25 per cent below the 911, putting it almost on a par with the departing 356. This proved a very successful package, and 1966 sales figures showed that the 912 accounted for almost two thirds of total 911/912 series production. The Targa body was also available on the 912, and in fact there was very little to distinguish the four-cylinder cars externally from the six-cylinder ones, other than the small '912' badge in the centre of the engine cover, and of course the less distinctive exhaust note.

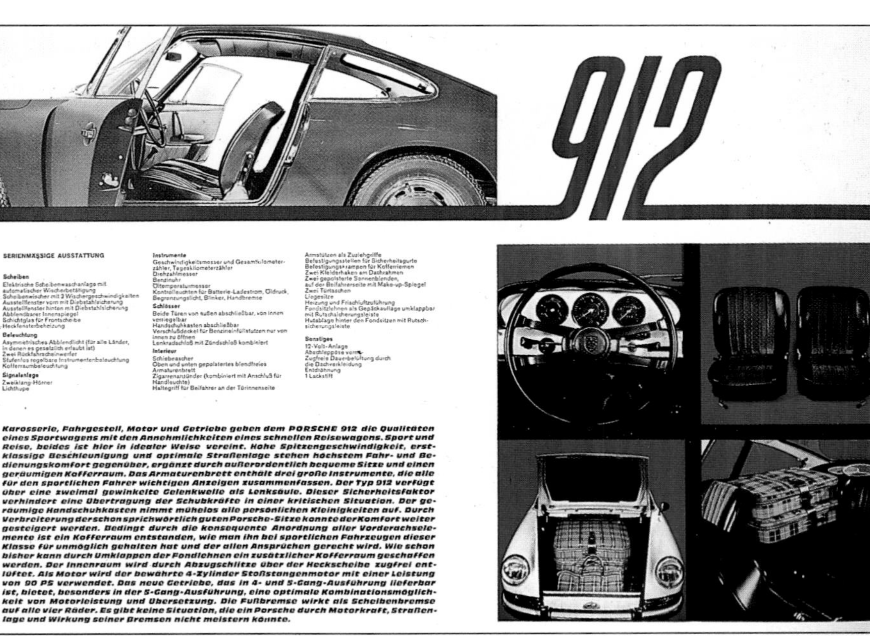

As improvements were made to the 911, so they also fed across to the 912, mainly as production economies. In 1967, the five-dial dashboard from the 911 was standardized across the range, replacing the previous 356-oriented three-dial in the 912. This gave the 912 driver oil pressure and water temperature gauges, plus a clock. With the suspension improvements mentioned earlier, he also got 911-style handling and greater safety. Although the gap in performance was not immense when the cars were introduced – 116mph (188kph) top speed/18 second standing quarter mile for the 912 against 125mph (202kph)/16 seconds correspondingly for the 911 – by 1970 the performance of the 912 had barely changed whereas the 911S was then boasting 140mph (227kph)/14.4 seconds. This inevitably reduced demand, and the 912 was dropped. It was revived in 1976 as the 912E, using the Volkswagen fuel-injected 2-litre engine from the 914 series, but was dropped again after one year.

914

The 914 was probably the most controversial Porsche ever produced. It is still not accepted as a true member of the marque, although rarity is now beginning to escalate prices of good examples. Perhaps the design was doomed from the start, because it was an early example of a joint venture and, consequently, had to satisfy too many separate requirements. We have seen that Porsche were always keen to retain an entry-level priced vehicle and had produced the 912 for some years. However, the constant development of that vehicle alongside the 911 continued to drive its price upwards and in the late 1960s the need arose for another model priced below the 912 which would not interfere with existing production arrangements. At the same time, Volkswagen were looking for a more sporting model to widen the appeal of their range and to replace the lack-lustre Karmann-Ghia sports model. Karmann were also in need of a new model to fill their spare production capacity. Hans Nordhoff, the head of VW, and Ferry Porsche met and came up with the ideal solution for all requirements.

Porsche would design a sports car capable of accepting a new 1.7-litre VW engine or the Porsche flat-six. Karmann would produce the bodies and assemble the VW-engined version, to be dubbed a 'VW-Porsche' in Europe but marketed as a Porsche in the USA, and sell bodies directly to Porsche for assembly as the larger-engined version.

Porsche already knew of an existing design study by a nearby company, Gugelot GmbH, for a front-engined sports car made out of advanced composite materials.

This was acquired and quickly adapted by 'Butzi' Porsche to accept either engine in a mid-mounted arrangement similar to Porsche's racing models.

RIGHT, 1970: *Unfortunately, during the design phase, Hans Nordhoff died. The agreements between VW and Porsche had been mainly verbal, and Kurt Lotz, the new Director of VW, changed some of the terms of these agreements. The result was a new marketing organization jointly owned by VW and Porsche, and a higher body price from Karmann to supply Porsche with fully trimmed and painted bodies rather than the plain bodyshells which Porsche wanted. The new VW-Porsche 914 appeared in 1970 to a less than rapturous reception. It was an outright two-seater with a mid-mounted VW 1.7-litre, flat-four air-cooled engine. The body featured a Targa-style roll-over bar and lift-out roof section. It was quite low, in fact a full 4 inches (10cm) lower than a 911, and to maintain the regulation headlamp height, pop-up units were used. The rear deck was very flat, and this, if anything, was the main reason for most objections, as it gave the impression that the styling budget had run-out just aft of the roll-over bar.*

Another advantage derived from the no-compromise concept of this car - two exceptionally large luggage compartments.

The 210 litre (7.4 cu. ft) luggage compartment at the front of the VW-Porsche is surprising enough for a sports car.

But to find another luggage compartment of no less than 250 litres (8.8 cu. ft) capacity at the rear is something quite out of the ordinary.

And competition for quite a few medium-sized family saloons.

Nor are these two luggage compartments suitable only for plastic bags filled with water! You can easily carry quite bulky objects when the need arises.

You needn't worry too much about scratching valuable items, either. Both luggage compartments are fully carpeted. Not just for appearance' sake, but to ensure that your suitcases finish the journey as presentable as they started out.

To conclude, a further advantage of two luggage compartments: you can load the car to an equal extent at front and rear. Thus making sure that nothing can upset the finely balanced neutral handling of this car.

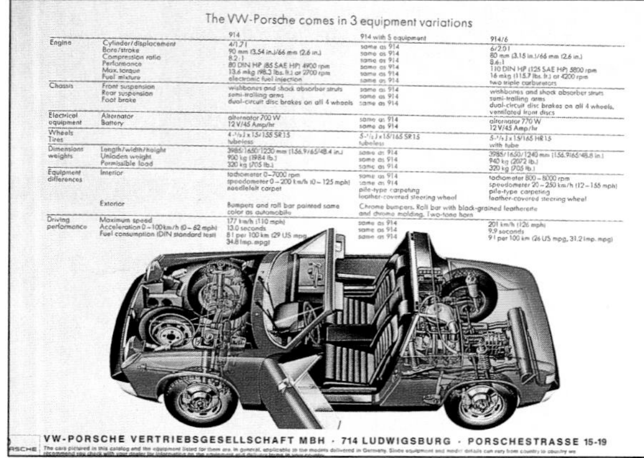

The VW-Porsche comes in 3 equipment variations

		914	914 with S equipment	914/6
Engine	Cylinder/displacement	4/1.7 l	same as 914	6/2.0 l
	Bore/stroke	90 mm (3.54 in.)/66 mm (2.6 in.)	same as 914	80 mm (3.15 in.)/66 mm (2.6 in.)
	Compression ratio	8.2:1	same as 914	8.6:1
	Performance	80 DIN HP (85 SAE HP) 4900 rpm	same as 914	110 DIN HP (125 SAE HP) 5800 rpm
	Max. torque	13.6 mkg (98.3 lbs. ft.) at 2700 rpm	same as 914	16 mkg (115.7 lbs. ft.) at 4200 rpm
	Fuel mixture	electronic fuel injection	same as 914	two triple carburetors
Chassis	Front suspension	wishbones and shock absorber struts	same as 914	wishbones and shock absorber struts
	Rear suspension	semi-trailing arms	same as 914	semi-trailing arms
	Foot brake	dual-circuit disc brakes on all 4 wheels	same as 914	dual-circuit disc brakes on all 4 wheels, ventilated front discs
Electrical equipment	Alternator	alternator 700 W	same as 914	alternator 770 W
	Battery	12 V/45 Amp/hr	same as 914	12 V/45 Amp/hr
Wheels Tires		4-½J x 15/155 SR 15 tubeless	5-½J x 15/165 SR 15 tubeless	5-½J x 15/165 HR 15 with tube
Dimensions weights	Length/width/height	3985/1650/1230 mm (156.9/65/48.4 in.)	same as 914	3985/1650/1240 mm (156.9/65/48.8 in.)
	Unladen weight	900 kg (1984 lb.)	same as 914	940 kg (2072 lb.)
	Permissible load	320 kg (705 lb.)	same as 914	320 kg (705 lb.)
Equipment differences	Interior	tachometer 0–7000 rpm speedometer 0–200 km/h (0–125 mph) needlefelt carpet	same as 914 same as 914 pile-type carpeting leather-covered steering wheel	tachometer 800–8000 rpm speedometer 20–250 km/h (12–155 mph) pile-type carpeting leather-covered steering wheel
	Exterior	Bumpers and roll bar painted same color as automobile	Chrome bumpers. Roll bar with black-grained leatherette and chrome molding. Two-tone horn	
Driving performance	Maximum speed	177 km/h (110 mph)	same as 914	201 km/h (126 mph)
	Acceleration 0–100 km/h (0–62 mph)	13.0 seconds	same as 914	9.9 seconds
	Fuel consumption (DIN standard test)	8 l per 100 km (29 US mpg, 34.8 Imp. mpg)	same as 914	9 l per 100 km (26 US mpg, 31.2 Imp. mpg)

VW-PORSCHE VERTRIEBSGESELLSCHAFT MBH · 714 LUDWIGSBURG · PORSCHESTRASSE 15-19

The cars pictured in this catalog and the equipment listed for them are, in general, applicable to the models delivered in Germany. Since equipment and model details can vary from country to country we

LEFT, 1970/1: *Both the five-speed gearbox and the suspension design – MacPherson struts at the front and longitudinal torsion bars at the rear – were pure Porsche. In fact, it was virtually identical to the 911, except that no anti-roll bars were used. Disc brakes were fitted all round and the basic car ran on 15-inch (37.5cm) diameter steel wheels.*

ABOVE, 1974: *The mid-mounting of the engine gave a more balanced 46/54 per cent front/rear weight distribution, and some 10 per cent superior to the 911 according to Porsche.*

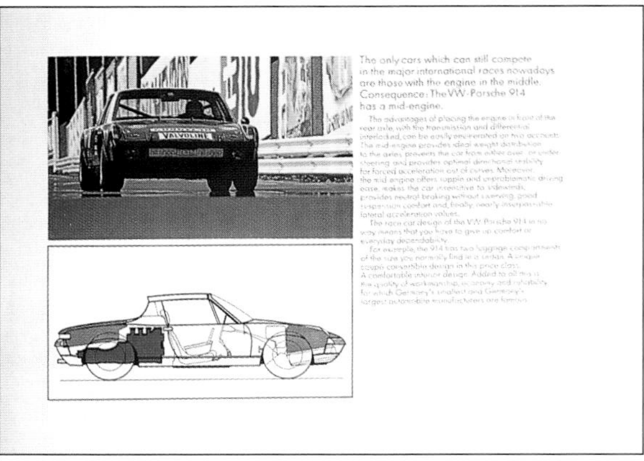

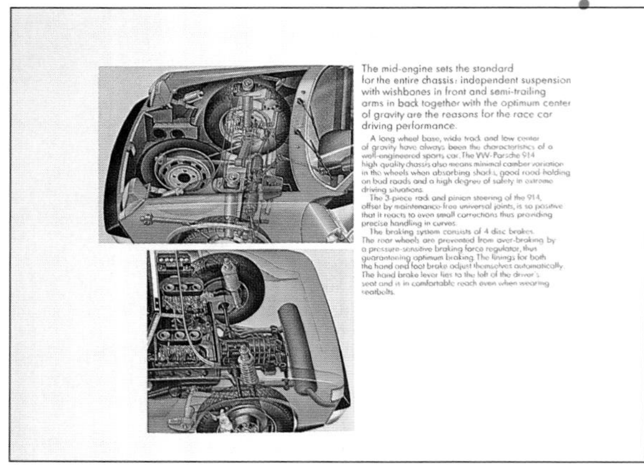

TOP AND ABOVE, 1974: *Despite the indifferent reception when it was announced, the 914/4, as the VW-engined version was dubbed, sold over 120,000 units between 1970 and 1975. Porsche themselves were not that happy with the car, and later in 1970 announced a 6-cylinder variant, the 914/6, utilizing the 2-litre engine from the 1969 911T.*

RIGHT, 1970: *Although the 914/6 retained the somewhat austere interior of the smaller-engined model, it was more generously equipped, being fitted with ventilated front discs, 911-style instrumentation, three-speed wipers, electric washers, headlamp flasher and two-tone horns.*

Full load performance – 914/6 engine

Output Ne (HP)
Torque Md (mkp)
Engine speed n (rpm)
Ne
Md
Ne max = 110 HP (DIN) at 5800 rpm
Md max = 16.0 mkp (115.7 lb/ft) at 4200 rpm

The 914/6 engine accelerates the car from 0 to 100 kph (62 mph) in 9.9 seconds. Top speed in this case is 201 kph (125 mph).

The air-cooled 6-cylinder engine with its 2 triple choke downdraught carburettors is mounted in the mid-engine position in front of the rear axle, and combined with clutch, gearbox and final drive to form a single unit.

Overhead valves in hemispherical combustion chambers are operated by rockers from a single overhead camshaft for each bank of cylinders. This engine has been designed from scratch as a high-performance power unit capable of running freely up to high speeds, and possessing enormous output reserves. Despite the fact that it develops 110 HP (DIN), it is rated conservatively enough to ensure quite exceptional strength and reliability.

The forged crankshaft runs in eight main bearings.

Great care has been taken to ensure an even supply of oil to all lubrication points even during rapid cornering. The oil is purified by a full flow oil filter, and maintained at a constant temperature by a thermostatically controlled oil cooler.

The chassis and running gear has been matched to the higher performance, with many strengthened components. For example, the front brakes have ventilated discs, wider rims are specified and high-speed tyres fitted.

The 914/6 instruments are more comprehensive. The screenwipers, for example, have three operating speeds,

ABOVE, 1974: *Externally, the 914/6 had chromed bumpers, wider steel or optional ten-spoke alloy wheels. The roll-over bar was vinyl-covered and additional chrome trim strips were also fitted. The 914/6 was some 70 per cent more expensive than the 914/4 and only slightly less than a base 911. Demand was poor and only 3,300 were produced before the 914/6 was dropped in 1972. In the end, the 914 was killed off by the fact that it tried to please too many masters, and ended up satisfying none. Demand was not high enough to justify development by VW, who were, after all, a volume producer. The styling was always a problem, attracting barbed comments from road testers who described it as 'a pleasant eyesore' and 'having the fluidity of line of an erector set'.*

916

Despite the failure of the 914 to appeal to a larger audience, Porsche had considered giving the car some development, and the result was the 916. This model very nearly got into production, but in the end was dropped just before it was due to be officially announced, mainly because of misgivings over the price, which was expected to be on a par with the Ferrari Dino.

These pictures were taken from a 1971 road test and show that the body was basically 914, but with a fixed roof and flared wheelarches. The front and rear bumpers were replaced by colour-keyed integral fibreglass sections. Under the engine cover was the 2.4-litre 190bhp flat-six from the 911S, and the suspension featured gas-filled shock absorbers and anti-roll bars front and rear. The interior was more luxurious and featured a leather/cloth trim and additional equipment such as the stereo radio/tape player.

EVER SINCE THE Porsche 914 and 914/6s arrived on the automotive scene, much has been rumored in the way of restyling the controversial lines of the car. One-offs have shown up at a number of the European shows and rumors of a newly revamped car based on the 914 series have been circulating for months. The first indication on the part of the Porsche works that a new car was being considered came last August when a variation on the 914 was seen at the factory. Reports had it that this car, and several others like it, were "special order cars for the Paris distributor." Then, in early October, photos of what was designated the Porsche 916 were circulated to all the U.S. distributors. Rather than being a restyled 914 or 914/6 residing in the $3400 to $6000 price bracket, the 916 was a super-luxurious 914/6 at a price rumored to be in the $14,000 to $15,000 bracket—or in other words, a 914/6 for the price of a Ferrari Dino. With the current money stabilization problems, the duty surcharge on imported cars, and the higher labor costs in manufacturing a low volume car, Porsche decided that the market wasn't large enough to warrant production. What is (or was) the 916 and how could it differ so much from the 914/6 so as to justify the price differential of $8000?

The 916 pictured here is the only "Americanized" 916 to

decision not to market the car here and was obtained by Peter Gregg of Brumos Porsche/Audi in Jacksonville, Fla. At first appearance, the 916 looks like the 914/6 GT that was campaigned last year in a number of FIA endurance races. The flared fenders are the same, the wider grille mesh over the engine compartment is the same and the front mounted oil cooler is included; however, after a closer look, one notices the small luxurious touches that indicate that this car was intended for highway use. The interior is upholstered in real honest-to-goodness leather. The instrument panel is lifted straight out of the standard 914/6 with the exception of the lefthand instrument group. There, an oil temperature gauge and oil pressure gauge have replaced the fuel gauge and idiot lights of the 914; the fuel gauge resides in a small center console. The seats have a rather mod fabric insert and, unlike the earlier 914 series, both seats are adjustable. A nice American touch, which seems likely for production, is a hidden radio antenna imbedded in the windshield. The antenna on this particular model was connected to a Becker AM/FM signal-seeking radio that features a cassette slot for stereo fans (not cartridge, mind you, but the latest cassette). The car isn't air conditioned, although Peter Gregg says it could be without much trouble. Probably the least noticeable but most significant styling/engineering fea-

strength of the car and in addition permits a sewn-in headliner with sound deadening material superior to the production 914s.

Mechanically the 916 has borrowed much from the production 1972 model 911s. It has the 2.4-liter, 190-bhp (net) engine and, like all 1972 Porsche 911s, the 916 will run on regular fuel. The engine drives through a 5-speed gearbox with the newly revised shifting pattern, i.e., the first four gears are in the standard "H" pattern with fifth gear to the far right and forward. Also new are the 7-in.-wide alloy wheels under those flared fenders. With the alloy wheels and the fiberglass "bumpers" front and rear, a savings of 70 lb over the production 914/6 has been realized. While on the subject of bumpers, the revised front and rear panels on the prototype are of fiberglass and would be hard pressed (no pun intended) to pass any collision test; however, one wonders if on a production model they might not have used a color-keyed rubber or polyurethane bumper.

The suspension features heavy-duty Bilstein shocks, anti-roll bars front and rear, and four ventilated disc brakes, again borrowed from the production 911S.

Gregg, whose expertise with Porsches of all varieties is widely recognized, did the chauffeuring duties for my ride in the 916. It is in the hands of an experienced driver that the value of this car is most evident. The car started and idled easily. The 2.4-liter engine is remarkably docile, considering that it is Porsche's highest-output production engine. It accelerates strongly and smoothly: not a real kick in the back like a big-displacement car but an authoritative shove back into the seat. The factory figures show a 0-60 mph time of "less than seven seconds" and although there was no time to run acceleration tests properly, there's reason to believe the factory figures are very conservative.

The 916 cornered flat and neutral throughout the speed range. Several 90-100-mph corners were negotiated close to the limit and, unlike the 911 series, the 916 did not require constant steering correction to maintain the line. Braking was straight and sure with no lockup. The Michelin XVR tires were a definite contributing factor to cornering ability at elevated speeds (these tires are standard equipment on the Citroen SM, Ferrari Daytona Coupe, and Porsche 911S) and were relatively quiet although they did emit a slight hum, more noticeable outside the car than inside. As in the production 914s the seats were comfortable. It did seem unfortunate on a car of this type that Audi-type inertia reels weren't used, as the belts are hard to adjust and have a tendency to flop out the door on exiting.

From a practical standpoint, Porsche's decision to not produce and market the 916 probably was the right one. But the 916 is a mechanical masterpiece, and one can't help but wish that the fortunate few who can afford $15,000 for such a car had been given the chance to own one.

BY BILL WARNER
PHOTOS BY THE AUTHOR

Do you want a luxurious 914/6 with 911S engine? Too bad. What you see is what you can't get.

FEBRUARY 1972 25

PORSCHE 916

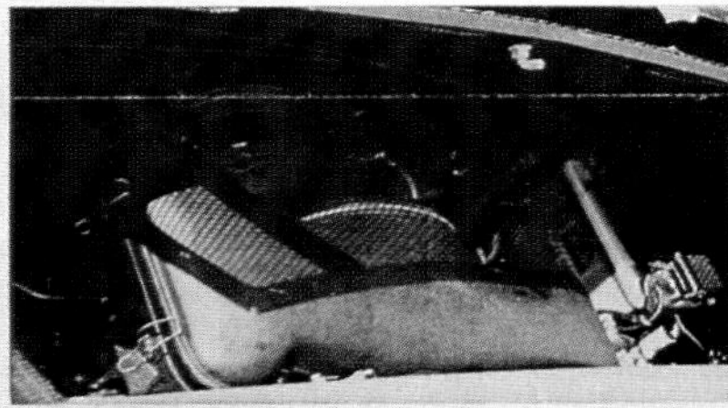

911S engine, 911S instrumentation, rich carpet, Becker radio, leather upholstery with print cloth inserts distinguish the 916 from a 914/6 along with the wild bodywork.

Engine:

Type	sohc flat 6
Bore x stroke, mm.	84.0 x 70.4
Equivalent in.	3.31 x 2.77
Displacement, cc/cu in.	2341/143
Bhp @ rpm	190 @ 6500
Torque @ rpm	159 @ 5200
Compression ratio	8.5:1
Fuel injection	Bosch mechanical
Type fuel required	regular, 91-oct
Emission control	fuel injection

Drive train:

Transmission	5-speed manual
Gear ratios: 5th (0.759)	3.36:1
4th (0.962)	4.26:1
3rd (1.26)	5.58:1
2nd (1.83)	8.10:1
1st (3.18)	14.06:1
Final drive ratio	4.43:1

Chassis & Body:

Body/frame .... unit steel
Brake type: vented disc; 11.1-in. front, 11.4-in. rear, vacuum assisted
Wheels .... alloy spoke, 15 x 7K
Tires .... Michelin XVR 185/70-15
Steering type .... rack & pinion
Front suspension: MacPherson struts, lower A-arms, torsion bars, tube shocks, anti-roll bar
Rear suspension: semi-trailing arms, coil springs, tube shocks anti-roll bar

General:

Curb weight, lb.	2000
Wheelbase, in.	96.4
Track, front/rear	54.6/58.3
Overall length	156.9
Width	68.3
Height	48.0
Ground Clearance	5.1
Overhang, front/rear	30.9/29.6
Fuel tank capacity, U.S. gal.	16.4

Acceleration from 0–60mph was quoted by the factory as being 'under seven seconds' which was probably conservative as usual. In the end, 20 prototype examples were built, which again shows how close this car came to production. Whether it would have sold or not we will never know, but it demonstrates that, given the opportunity, even the ugliest duckling can aspire to being a swan.

924

When reviewing the history of the Porsche 924, it is not difficult to have a feeling of *deja vu*, because quite a number of factors leading to its introduction are similar to previous models. The result, however, was the most 'different' Porsche to date, a fact which once again brought criticism from the *cogniscenti*. As usual, the criticism was misplaced and the 924 evolved not only in its own right, but also to form the basis of the 944, the car that would ultimately give Porsche a genuine alternative to the 911 format.

Porsche had already embarked on the development of a new luxury car of their own, the 928, which they hoped would eventually replace the 911. The marketing men wanted some technical and family resemblances to this car as well, so it can be seen that the design brief was quite challenging.

It did not take long after its launch for the new VW-Porsche joint marketing company to realize that the 914 did not have the hoped for sales potential. As early as 1970, plans were under discussion for a replacement, but this time the car would be designed by Porsche and would be marketed as an Audi, using as many existing VW components as practicable. Other requirements were that the car should be front-engined to allow for a 2+2 seating arrangement with higher levels of comfort and reasonable boot capacity.

By 1973, considerable progress had been made. As air-cooled engines were being phased-out by VW, one of their new family of water-cooled units was selected, the source of which would prove to be an easy target for critics.

At this point, VW chief Rudolph Leiding decided to disband the joint marketing arrangements, and as VW had funded all development on the car to that point, he announced that it would be marketed purely through existing VW/Audi outlets. Porsche were dismayed by this development, as it meant that once production of the 914 finished, they would have no lower market sector model for their own dealers. However, the arrival of a former Ford man, Tony Schmucker, as replacement for Leiding together with the energy crunch of 1974, brought swift changes.

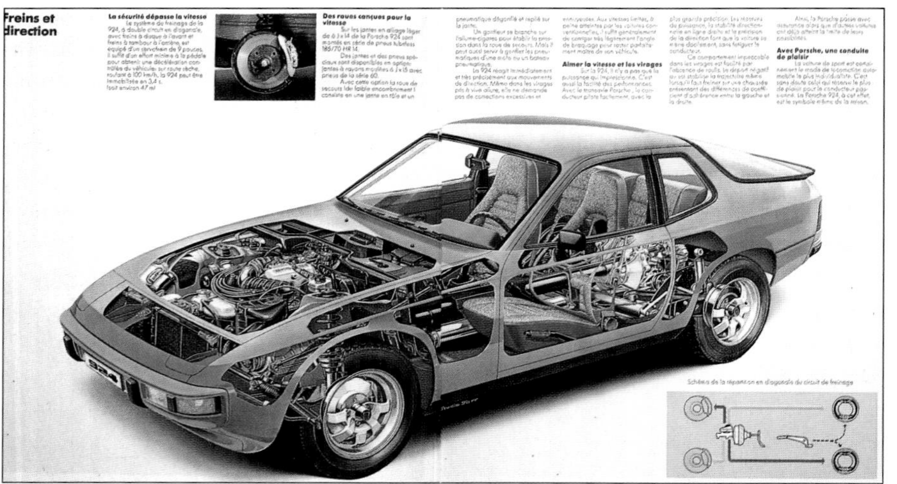

LEFT, 1984: *Most of the design was by this time settled, including the engine choice. The 2-litre, 4-cylinder engine had a single belt-driven overhead camshaft, with heron-type crossflow cylinder head (meaning that the head surface was flat with the combustion chambers set into the top of the pistons). It would use Bosch K-Jetronic Fuel Injection, all very state-of-the-art.*

RIGHT, 1981/82: *VW management decided that they had no place in their plans for a sports car and cancelled the project, having already spent $70m on its development. Porsche, however, had already realized the potential for their design and negotiated the purchase of the design and production rights for the car at a slightly discounted price. This was offset by the need for the car to be assembled at the Audi/NSU Neckarsulm plant to the north of Stuttgart, a necessity for Porsche as their own facilities were at full capacity to meet demand for the 911 and create launch stocks for the 928.*

Brakes, Steering:

A close relationship within the Porsche family.

With its exceptional power-to-weight ratio, just 18.05 lbs. per hp, Porsche 924 Turbo is one of a select breed of sports cars on the road today. At the same time, it is also designed for safety. This is based in part on an outstanding brake system. Matched to the sporting chassis, the sure, effective brakes let the driver experience effortless power while retaining full confidence in his ability to stop within a reasonable distance. This confidence is fully justified since the brakes in Porsche 924 Turbo bear a close resemblance to those of the 911SC and 928.

Numerous components tested in the 911SC and 928 have been adopted for the 924 Turbo. In addition to rugged wheel bearings, these include a five-bolt wheel-fastening system and the hydraulic dual-diagonal brake system. Four floating caliper disc brakes help tame Porsche 924 Turbo's high power, providing a very comforting 60 to 0 stopping distance, at light load and on a dry road, of just 148 feet.

All four brake discs are internally ventilated to prevent fading during hard braking. As in the 928 and 911, the parking brake operates through separate drums on the two rear wheels.

To accommodate its larger brakes, 924 Turbo is equipped with 15-inch wheel rims. They carry high-speed radials, size 185/70VR15.

The dual-circuit diagonal brake system of the 924, with disc brakes in front and drums at the rear, utilizes the same 9-inch power booster as the Turbo. A light pressure on the pedal brings the car sensitively to a halt. From 60 mph at light load and on a dry road, the 924 can come to a dead stop in 148 feet.

Reliable radials.

Tubeless radial tires, size 185/70 HR14 are mounted as standard equipment on the 6J x 14 light-alloy rims of the Porsche 924.

For both 924 models, special sizes can be obtained at additional cost: cast 6J x 15 spoke wheels with Series 60 radials for the 924; 6J x 16 forged wheels with 205/55VR16 low profile radials for the 924 Turbo.

Holding its course.

Sheer power, plus the ease with which it is used, combine to make Porsche 924 such an impressive sports car. The transaxle Porsche makes precision driving easy. Its high output, reassuring road-holding capability, and precise steering mean that the vehicle imposes few demands on the driver.

The 924 responds with accuracy to every movement of the steering wheel. Even when taken through a curving course at high speeds by an experienced driver, the car requires little or no correction. At speeds barely reached by conventional automobiles, all that is normally needed to keep the 924 on course is a slight movement of the wheel.

The ability to hold the road in tight curves is aided by the absence of troublesome body roll. Complementing this characteristic is negative steering roll radius, an advanced suspension geometry that helps the driver maintain directional control, even when front-tire roll resistance varies. This is particularly important when braking on uneven surfaces or stopping with a blow out.

With Porsche, driving has always been and will always be fun.

Driving a sports car is probably the most individual means of locomotion, and undoubtedly the one that gives the greatest pleasure to the enthusiastic driver. In Porsche 924, the driver can find a rational basis for this enjoyment.

20

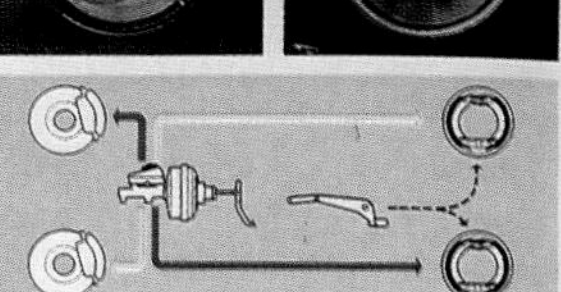

BELOW, 1981: *This gave an almost equal 48/52 per cent front/rear weight distribution which in turn produced near neutral handling. The gearbox was initially four-speed, with an optional automatic which used the then-new Audi three-speed unit. Most of the braking system and suspension was derived from VW/Audi parts originating from all sorts of vehicles, including the Golf, Beetle, K70 and even the Type 181 Utility vehicle (better known as 'The Thing'). Nevertheless, it all worked remarkably well and the car was well received by road testers.*

ABOVE, 1981: *What had not been decided at this stage was the transmission arrangement. Front wheel drive had been considered. There was a VW front-wheel drive transmission package in the new Audi 100 which would have fitted the bill nicely. Now that the car was to be a Porsche, however, family ties came into play, and it was decided to follow the same pattern as the new 928 model by using rear-wheel drive with the gearbox also placed at the rear in unit with the final drive.*

ABOVE, 1985: *The body design was entirely Porsche, being conceived by a Dutch member of the internal design staff, Harm Lagaay. Despite the engine being water-cooled, the company decided on the familiar grille-less nose shape, and cooling air was drawn in through a large duct under the front bumper. To keep the bonnetline low, the engine was installed at an angle of 40 degrees and pop-up headlights were used. At the rear, a large compound-curved rear window formed a hatchback which gave access to a larger luggage compartment than previously offered on any Porsche. At the time of introduction, the cars cd value of 0.36 was the best on any car in the world.*

LEFT, 1985: *In true Porsche fashion, development produced yearly improvements to the car. A five-speed gearbox was offered first as an option, and then standard from 1979, by which time the 924 accounted for 60 per cent of Porsche's output. A turbocharged version arrived in 1980 and then in 1982 the 944 arrived. This new model immediately began to take sales from the 924 and so in 1986, as a final filip for the 924, the 2.5-litre 944 engine was installed to create the 924S. The basic specification included tinted glass, electric windows, power steering and air conditioning. Performance was good as well, with 134mph (217kph) top speed, compared to the original car's 110mph (178kph), and acceleration from 0–60mph of just over 8 seconds. Nevertheless, it still did not have the appeal of the 944, and demand was not great, 924 production finally ceasing in 1988.*

BELOW, 1981: *In response to some customer complaints about the mediocre performance of the basic 924, Porsche introduced a turbocharged version in 1980. The main external distinguishing features were the four oblong cooling slots in the nose section just above the bumper, a NACA-duct on the right side of the bonnet and the exclusive 'spiders-web' alloy wheels. An unusual two-tone paint finish was also used on some of the early models.*

PORSCHE 924 – Une voiture de sport d'une grande habitabilité.

Conçues comme des coupés sport compacts et maniables, les Porsche 924 et 924 Turbo, surprennent par leur grande habitabilité. Deux enfants voyagent à l'aise sur les sièges arrières, et un ou deux adultes peuvent y prendre place pour des trajets moins longs.

Il y a aussi assez de place pour des bagages volumineux, voire encombrants. Le large hayon permet un chargement et un déchargement faciles. Il suffit de rabattre les dossiers des sièges arrières pour augmenter le volume du coffre de 370 litres et transformer ainsi cette voiture de sport en un véhicule idéal pour le travail, les loisirs, les vacances et les achats.

Un cache bagages à enrouleur protège le contenu du coffre des regards indiscrets et des rayons du soleil. Dans la 924, un jerrycan de secours, triangle de pré-signalisation et accessoires indispensables, si difficiles à loger dans beaucoup de voitures, disparaissent dans des compartiments latéraux, profonds, dissimulés sous le tapis du coffre.

Even the 924 Turbo, possib the fastest production 2-litre in th world, scorns change of shape an the incorporation of "exciting" styling. Its only exterior difference are limited to two minor changes which are directly due to the in- crease in power and its effect or speed and road-holding.

The new styling of the in- creased diameter 15" alloy whee permits the installation of a brakin system incorporating four inter- nally ventilated disc brakes in keeping with the greater perfor- mance.

The grilles, left and right o the front spoiler, provide addition cooling for the front brakes and th oil cooler. The additional air intake between the front headlights – an one NACA* opening (direct from motor racing) to the right of the front bonnet – take care of the cooling and the extraction of hot air from the engine compartmen

A small polyurethane rear spoiler, integral with the rear window frame, lowers the wind resistance factor from a creditab 0.36 to 0.35, and limits high spee lift while enhancing the grip of the driven wheels and directiona stability.

*NACA – National Advisory Committee for Aeronau

BELOW, 1981: *Other changes included twin fuel pumps and ventilated disc brakes all round. Virtually everything in the transmission and suspension departments was beefed-up to handle what was a quite substantial power and performance increase.*

Fahren, das Spaß macht: im Porsche

Sportwagenfahren ist wohl die individuellste Art der motorisierten Fortbewegung und zweifellos diejenige, die einem engagierten Fahrer am meisten Vergnügen bereitet – auf leerer Landstraße ebenso wie in der Stadt oder auf der Autobahn.

Natürlich ist ein Porsche anderen Verkehrsteilnehmern überlegen – weniger infolge seiner hohen Spitzengeschwindigkeit als vielmehr durch Spurtkraft und damit seinem Vorteil beim Überholen auf kurzer Distanz, seiner sicheren Straßen- und Kurvenlage, seinem kurzen Bremsweg, seinem spontanen Ansprechen auf Lenkbewegungen und seiner begeisternden Handlichkeit.

Im Porsche 924 erfolgt die Beschleunigung von Null auf Hundert mit dem serienmäßigen Fünfganggetriebe in 9,6 s und mit der komfortablen Vollautomatic in 11,4 s. Die Spitze von 200 km/h wird mit Schaltgetriebe leicht über-, mit Automatic leicht unterschritten.

Mit seiner spezifischen Motorleistung von 65,5 kW (89,2 PS) pro Liter Hubraum benötigt der Turbo für den Sprint vom Stillstand auf 100 km/h ganze 7,7 s; seine Höchstgeschwindigkeit beträgt 230 km/h, und 1000 m aus dem Stand schafft er in 27,9 s.

ABOVE, 1981: *The entire car was assembled at Porsche's works at Zuffenhausen. As well as the KKK turbocharger, the engine received a new cylinder head, pistons, inlet and exhaust manifolds. In fact only the basic block remained interchangeable with the standard car.*

ABOVE, 1981: *In the European version, 170bhp was now on tap, compared to the standard car's 110bhp, and this not only lowered the 0–60mph acceleration time by over 4 seconds, to just under 7 seconds, but also raised the top speed to over 140mph (227kph). Turbo-lag, a flat spot normally experienced on turbocharged cars at low revs prior to full boost being available from the turbocharger, was apparent but not as marked as on similar models from other manufacturers.*

LEFT AND RIGHT, 1980/1: *To further promote this new, muscular image for the 924, the name Carrera was invoked again to adorn a limited run of customer racers based on the 924 Turbo. The 924 Carrera GT featured a further uprating of the engine to 210bhp along with competition suspension and transmission modifications, including the use of 930 wheels and tyres.*

BELOW LEFT, 1980/1: *To accommodate these, the body sprouted flared plastic wheelarch extensions, plus additional aerodynamic aids such as the chin spoiler at the front and a rear spoiler on the lower edge of the tailgate. In fact, other than for the large airscoop on the right side of the bonnet, the Carrera GT firmly predicted the shape of the yet-to-be-announced 944.*

RIGHT, 1980/1: *A rally version, the Carrera GTS, was also built featuring 280bhp engine and alloy body panels, together with all the appropriate modifications for this type of motor sport.*

RIGHT, 1981: *The final fire-breathing version, the Carrera GTR, was an out-and-out circuit car with 375bhp available. Three of these cars competed at Le Mans in 1981, the leading one taking 11th place overall and winning the IMSA GTO category.*

BELOW, 1980/81: *Alas, the Le Mans model sold in 1981 bore no resemblance to the 924 GTR which raced that year. It was in fact a basic 924 with special paint scheme and fitted with the Turbo alloy wheels and other options as standard.*

Abweichend zur serienmäßigen Ausstattung des Porsche 924 ist der Porsche 924 »Le Mans« wie folgt ausgestattet:

● Lackierung und Dekor:
»Alpin-weiß« mit umlaufenden dreifarbigen Dekorstreifen
und »Le Mans«-Schriftzügen seitlich
Folien mit Schriftzügen »924« auf den Einstiegschwellern

● Innenausstattung:
Schwarzes Kunstleder mit Nadelstreifen-Stoff schwarz/weiß und weißen Kedern
4-Speichen-Lederlenkrad, 36 cm Ø

● Fahrwerk:
Sportstoßdämpfer
Stabilisatoren vorn und hinten

● Räder und Reifen:
Leichtmetall-Räder 6Jx15, schwarz pulverbeschichtet, mit blank übergedrehten Speichen
Reifen 205/60 HR 15

● Sonstiges:
Heckspoiler
Heckwischereinbau vorbereitet

The equipment of the 924 "Le Mans" differs from that of the standard Porsche 924 in the following details:

● Paintwork and finish:
"alpine-white" with three-colour decorative stripe all round and the "Le Mans" autograph on the sides
Foils with the "924" symbol on the doorsills

● Interior equipment:
Black leatherette with black/white pinstripe fabric and white borders
4-spoke steering wheel, leather-covered, 36 cm (14 in.) dia.

● Chassis:
Sporting shock absorbers
Anti-roll bars front and rear

● Wheels and tyres:
Light alloy wheels 6Jx15, black powder-coated with bright lathe-turned spokes
Tyres 205/60 HR 15

● General:
Rear spoiler
Provision for a rear screen wiper

A la différence de la version de série de la Porsche 924, la Porsche 924 «Le Mans» est équipée comme suit:

● Peinture et décoration:
«Blanc alpin» avec bandes décoratives et inscription «Le Mans» sur les côtes
Feuilles plastiques avec l'inscription «924» sur les seuils de portes

● Aménagement intérieur:
Simili-cuir noir avec étoffe velours tennis noir/blanc et bourrelets blancs
Volant à 4 branches, revêtu de cuir, 36 cm de Ø

● Châssis:
Amortisseurs de sport
Stabilisateurs à l'avant et à l'arrière

● Jantes et pneus:
Jantes en métal léger 6Jx15, revêtues de peinture en poudre noire, avec rayons finement polis
Pneus 205/60 HR 15

● Divers:
Becquet aérodynamique à l'arrière
Montage d'essui-glace arrière, préparé

Änderungen vorbehalten
Subject to change.
Sous réserve de modifications

Dr.Ing.h.c.F.Porsche
Aktiengesellschaft
Porschestrasse 42, 7000 Stuttgart 40

Printed in Germany, WVK 111813

ABOVE, 1980/81: *For some strange reason, the 924 was never a resounding hit with enthusiasts. Not that there was anything wrong with the design or its VW engine. This was first used, in carburated form, in the VW LT van, and it seems more the thought of a Porsche sports car with a water-cooled van engine at the front that made 'Porschephiles' shudder. But they were not being stupid, just demonstrating that old human trait of resistance to change.*

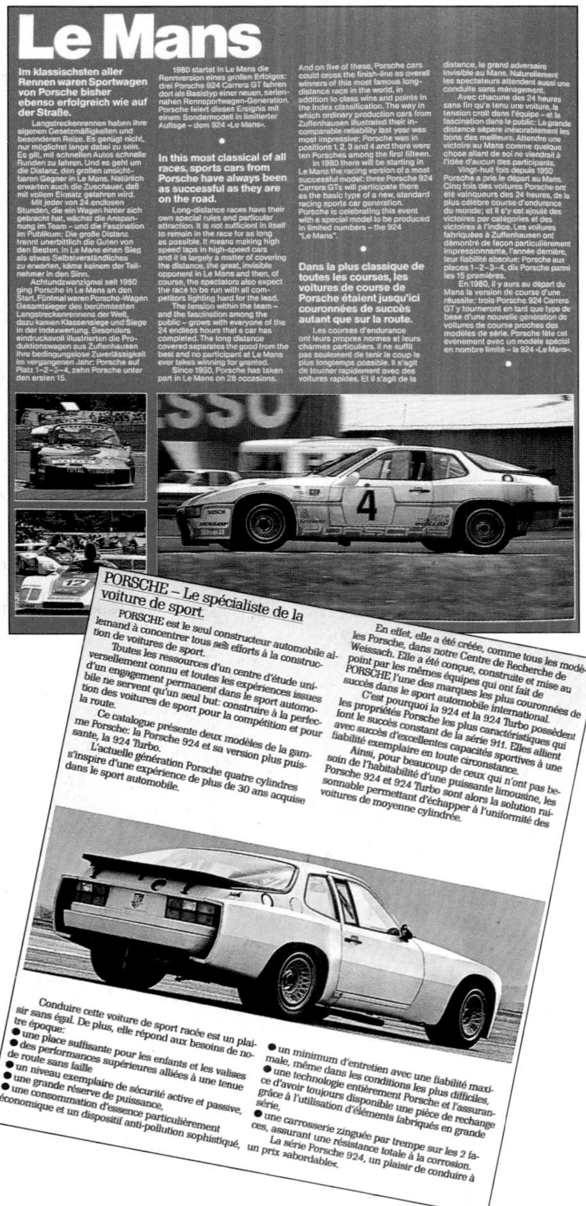

Le Mans

Im klassischsten aller Rennen waren Sportwagen von Porsche bisher ebenso erfolgreich wie auf der Straße.

Langstreckenrennen haben ihre eigenen Gesetzmäßigkeiten und besonderen Reize. Es genügt nicht, nur möglichst lange dabei zu sein. Es gilt, mit schnellen Autos schnelle Runden zu fahren. Und es geht um die Distanz, den großen unsichtbaren Gegner in Le Mans. Natürlich erwarten auch die Zuschauer, daß mit vollem Einsatz gefahren wird.

Mit jeder von 24 endlosen Stunden, die ein Wagen hinter sich gebracht hat, wächst die Anspannung im Team – und die Faszination im Publikum: Die große Distanz trennt unerbittlich die Guten von den Besten. In Le Mans einen Sieg als etwas Selbstverständliches zu erwarten, käme keinem der Teilnehmer in den Sinn.

Achtundzwanzigmal seit 1950 ging Porsche in Le Mans an den Start. Fünfmal waren Porsche-Wagen Gesamtsieger des berühmtesten Langstreckenrennens der Welt, dazu kamen Klassensiege und Siege in der Indexwertung. Besonders eindrucksvoll illustrierten die Produktionswagen aus Zuffenhausen ihre bedingungslose Zuverlässigkeit im vergangenen Jahr: Porsche auf Platz 1–2–3–4, zehn Porsche unter den ersten 15.

1980 startet in Le Mans die Rennversion eines großen Erfolges: drei Porsche 924 Carrera GT fahren dort als Basistyp einer neuen, seriennahen Rennsportwagen-Generation. Porsche feiert dieses Ereignis mit einem Sondermodell in limitierter Auflage – dem 924 »Le Mans«.

•

In this most classical of all races, sports cars from Porsche have always been as successful as they are on the road.

Long-distance races have their own special rules and particular attraction. It is not sufficient in itself to remain in the race for as long as possible. It means making high speed laps in high-speed cars and it is largely a matter of covering the distance, the great, invisible opponent in Le Mans and then, of course, the spectators also expect the race to be run with all competitors fighting hard for the lead.

The tension within the team – and the fascination among the public – grows with everyone of the 24 endless hours that a car has completed. The long distance covered separates the good from the best and no participant at Le Mans ever takes winning for granted.

Since 1950, Porsche has taken part in Le Mans on 28 occasions. And on five of these, Porsche cars could cross the finish-line as overall winners of this most famous long-distance race in the world, in addition to class wins and points in the Index classification. The way in which ordinary production cars from Zuffenhausen illustrated their incomparable reliability last year was most impressive: Porsche was in positions 1, 2, 3 and 4 and there were ten Porsches among the first fifteen.

In 1980 there will be starting in Le Mans the racing version of a most successful model: three Porsche 924 Carrera GTs will participate there as the basic type of a new, standard racing sports car generation. Porsche is celebrating this event with a special model to be produced in limited numbers – the 924 "Le Mans".

•

Dans la plus classique de toutes les courses, les voitures de course de Porsche étaient jusqu'ici couronnées de succès autant que sur la route.

Les courses d'endurance ont leurs propres normes et leurs charmes particuliers. Il ne suffit pas seulement de tenir le coup le plus longtemps possible. Il s'agit de tourner rapidement avec des voitures rapides. Et il s'agit de la distance, le grand adversaire invisible au Mans. Naturellement les spectateurs attendent aussi une conduite sans ménagement.

Avec chacune des 24 heures sans fin qu'a tenu une voiture, la tension croît dans l'équipe – et la fascination dans le public: La grande distance sépare inéxorablement les bons des meilleurs. Attendre une victoire au Mans comme quelque chose allant de soi ne viendrait à l'idée d'aucun des participants.

Vingt-huit fois depuis 1950 Porsche a pris le départ au Mans. Cinq fois des voitures Porsche ont été vainqueurs des 24 heures, de la plus célèbre course d'endurance du monde; et il s'y est ajouté des victoires par catégories et des victoires à l'indice. Les voitures fabriquées à Zuffenhausen ont démontré de façon particulièrement impressionnante, l'année dernière, leur fiabilité absolue: Porsche aux places 1–2–3–4, dix Porsche parmi les 15 premières.

En 1980, il y aura au départ du Mans la version de course d'une réussite: trois Porsche 924 Carrera GT y tourneront en tant que type de base d'une nouvelle génération de voitures de course proches des modèles de série. Porsche fête cet événement avec un modèle spécial en nombre limité – la 924 »Le Mans«.

•

PORSCHE – Le spécialiste de la voiture de sport.

PORSCHE est le seul constructeur automobile allemand à concentrer tous ses efforts à la construction de voitures de sport.

Toutes les ressources d'un centre d'étude universellement connu et toutes les expériences issues d'un engagement permanent dans le sport automobile ne servent qu'un seul but: construire à la perfection des voitures de sport pour la compétition et pour la route.

Ce catalogue présente deux modèles de la gamme Porsche: la Porsche 924 et sa version plus puissante, la 924 Turbo.

L'actuelle génération Porsche quatre cylindres s'inspire d'une expérience de plus de 30 ans acquise dans le sport automobile.

En effet, elle a été créée, comme tous les modèles Porsche, dans notre Centre de Recherche de Weissach. Elle a été conçue, construite et mise au point par les mêmes équipes qui ont fait de PORSCHE l'une des marques les plus couronnées de succès dans le sport automobile international.

C'est pourquoi la 924 et la 924 Turbo possèdent les propriétés Porsche les plus caractéristiques qui font le succès constant de la série 911. Elles allient avec succès d'excellentes capacités sportives à une fiabilité exemplaire en toute circonstance.

Ainsi, pour beaucoup de ceux qui n'ont pas besoin de l'habitabilité d'une puissante limousine, les Porsche 924 et 924 Turbo sont alors la solution raisonnable permettant d'échapper à l'uniformité des voitures de moyenne cylindrée.

Conduire cette voiture de sport racée est un plaisir sans égal. De plus, elle répond aux besoins de notre époque:
- une place suffisante pour les enfants et les valises
- des performances supérieures alliées à une tenue de route sans faille
- un niveau exemplaire de sécurité active et passive,
- une grande réserve de puissance,
- une consommation d'essence particulièrement économique et un dispositif anti-pollution sophistiqué,
- un minimum d'entretien avec une fiabilité maximale, même dans les conditions les plus difficiles,
- une technologie entièrement Porsche et l'assurance d'avoir toujours disponible une pièce de rechange grâce à l'utilisation d'éléments fabriqués en grande série,
- une carrosserie zinguée par trempe sur les 2 faces, assurant une résistance totale à la corrosion.

La série Porsche 924, un plaisir de conduire à un prix »abordable«.

LEFT, 1980/81: *One only has to visit a Porsche Owners meeting to realize that, although they all belong to the same somewhat exclusive club, there is a perfectly friendly rivalry between the two camps. The fact that Porsche themselves are able to keep both happy simultaneously is an indication of just how clever the men from Zuffenhausen really are.*

RIGHT, 1980/81: *What the 924 did was to place Porsche enthusiasts into two distinct camps. First there are the traditionalists who will go on buying the 911 series, and its derivatives, it seems forever. Secondly, there is an ever-growing band of 'new' enthusiasts who have been brought into the fold by the 924/944 series cars. These drivers would probably never tolerate the somewhat esoteric demands of a 911, but have been given a whole new set of parameters by which to judge Porsche excellence.*

944

Regardless of the 924's commercial success, it was thought that this model could never reach its full potential unless it became a true Porsche. This meant removing the unloved VW/Audi engine. The car that resulted from this line of thinking, the 944, was so successful in terms of image projection, that many of the lower-priced volume production sportscars mimmick all or part of its styling. This is not because they are in competition with the latest 944 – most are half the price – but because their most immediate competition is a used 944, which, because of its build quality, wears out and therefore depreciates less quickly than its lesser rivals. Buyers are often more intelligent than they are given credit for, and an increasing number make their entry into Porsche ownership by buying a good used example of the 944.

The new engine was a 2.5-litre water-cooled 4-cylinder unit, which appeared at first to be half of the V8 unit from the 928 models. This was not in fact the case, as there were no parts which could be interchanged between the two engines. Because new engines are not developed cheaply, Porsche utilized research which had already been carried out in development of the V8 engine as the basis for the new 4-cylinder unit. A single overhead camshaft operated just two valves per cylinder via hydraulic lifters. A Bosch DME engine management system was fitted and all of this produced 160bhp. One of the main criticisms of the VW/Audi engine was excessive vibration. This was solved on the new, and larger, engine by using twin balance shafts.

The new body was based on the 924 Carrera GT, but with all panels in steel. This provided more muscular and visually appealing styling. It also allowed for improvements to the suspension and the fitment of wider wheels.

The interior was virtually identical to the 924 other than for a different cloth trim. Standard equipment included tinted glass, electric windows, fog lights and remotely adjustable door mirrors. Options included air conditioning and sunroof, although the latter was a tilt/lift-out hatch type.

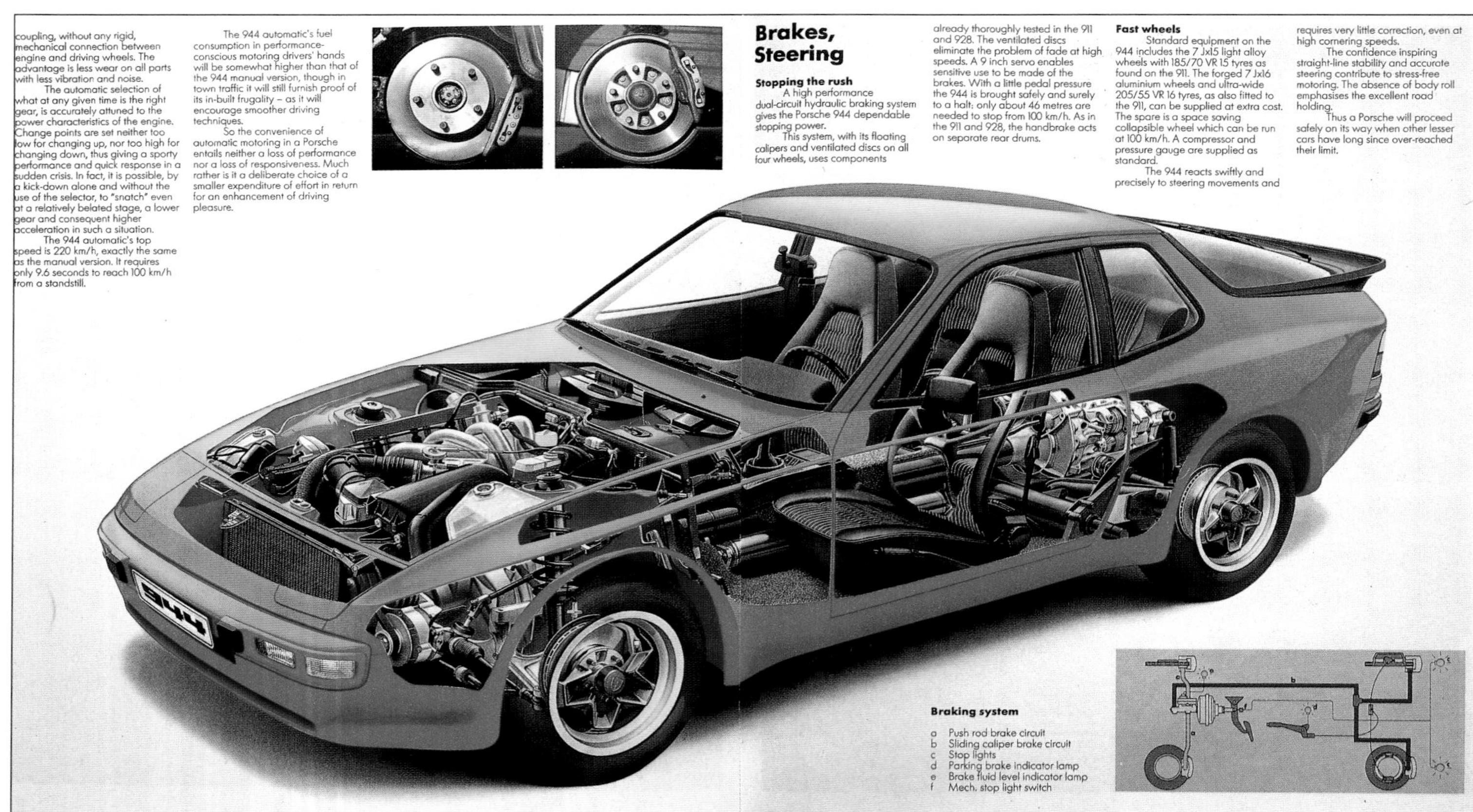

coupling, without any rigid, mechanical connection between engine and driving wheels. The advantage is less wear on all parts with less vibration and noise.

The automatic selection of what at any given time is the right gear, is accurately attuned to the power characteristics of the engine. Change points are set neither too low for changing up, nor too high for changing down, thus giving a sporty performance and quick response in a sudden crisis. In fact, it is possible, by a kick-down alone and without the use of the selector, to "snatch" even at a relatively belated stage, a lower gear and consequent higher acceleration in such a situation.

The 944 automatic's top speed is 220 km/h, exactly the same as the manual version. It requires only 9.6 seconds to reach 100 km/h from a standstill.

The 944 automatic's fuel consumption in performance-conscious motoring drivers' hands will be somewhat higher than that of the 944 manual version, though in town traffic it will still furnish proof of its in-built frugality – as it will encourage smoother driving techniques.

So the convenience of automatic motoring in a Porsche entails neither a loss of performance nor a loss of responsiveness. Much rather is it a deliberate choice of a smaller expenditure of effort in return for an enhancement of driving pleasure.

Brakes, Steering

Stopping the rush

A high performance dual-circuit hydraulic braking system gives the Porsche 944 dependable stopping power.

This system, with its floating calipers and ventilated discs on all four wheels, uses components already thoroughly tested in the 911 and 928. The ventilated discs eliminate the problem of fade at high speeds. A 9 inch servo enables sensitive use to be made of the brakes. With a little pedal pressure the 944 is brought safely and surely to a halt: only about 46 metres are needed to stop from 100 km/h. As in the 911 and 928, the handbrake acts on separate rear drums.

Fast wheels

Standard equipment on the 944 includes the 7 Jx15 light alloy wheels with 185/70 VR 15 tyres as found on the 911. The forged 7 Jx16 aluminium wheels and ultra-wide 205/55 VR 16 tyres, as also fitted to the 911, can be supplied at extra cost. The spare is a space saving collapsible wheel which can be run at 100 km/h. A compressor and pressure gauge are supplied as standard.

The 944 reacts swiftly and precisely to steering movements and requires very little correction, even at high cornering speeds.

The confidence inspiring straight-line stability and accurate steering contribute to stress-free motoring. The absence of body roll emphasises the excellent road holding.

Thus a Porsche will proceed safely on its way when other lesser cars have long since over-reached their limit.

Braking system

a Push rod brake circuit
b Sliding caliper brake circuit
c Stop lights
d Parking brake indicator lamp
e Brake fluid level indicator lamp
f Mech. stop light switch

ABOVE, 1983: *With a top speed of 130mph (211kph) and a 0–60mph time of 8.3 seconds, the 944 was an immediate success. The launch price was very competitive and there was very little to criticize. In fact, early road testers were so glowing in their praise as to leave some readers wondering whether they were reading a company press release.*

ABOVE, 1983: *But the praise was not misplaced, because as ever Porsche had done its homework, and done it well. Within a year of introduction it accounted for over half of Porsche's sales, although some of these were captured from the clearly overshadowed 924. In time-honoured fashion, development continued, and the 1986 models received a new interior, similar in concept to the 928, and a vast improvement on the somewhat plasticky 924 derivative.*

The comprehensive insulation and damping equipment absorbs high-frequency engine noise, prevents heat transfer from the engine compartment, damps vibrations of sheet metal and screens the interior from outside traffic noise.

The in-car audio system

Exacting standards of performance and expectations of luxury are well met by the stereo sound system. The Porsche 944 can be supplied, at extra cost, with two rear and one front stereo speaker, a balance control unit, radio interference suppression, electric or manually operated aerial as well as a tape cassette holder.

Apart from two stereo-cassette units, there is a choice of two digital stereo cassette radios, one with automatic traffic information decoder. On the digital model six frequencies can be programmed and push-button operated. The automatic electronic station seeker works in two directions and the frequency to which the set is tuned is shown on the digital display.

ABOVE, 1982/83: *The interior was trimmed with a new, more luxurious pinstripe cloth. New alloy wheels were also fitted, and then late in 1987, the engine was enlarged to 2.7 litres. The basic 944 model was discontinued in 1988, leaving the 944S as the 'entry-level' model.*

TURBOCHARGED POWER IN ABUNDANCE

The race developed turbocharger gives the 2.5 litre, 4-cylinder engine an output of 100 bhp/litre

By calling on their racing experience, the Porsche engineers have developed the 2.5 litre 4-cylinder turbo-charged engine to produce a remarkable 250 bhp DIN (184 kW) at 5,800 rpm, one of the few engines in the world to reach the 100 bhp per litre mark.

In Porsche's case, this achievement underlines performance rather than undermines reliability and with a maximum torque of 350 Nm at 4,000 rpm, the 944 Turbo possesses awesome reserves of power.

Capable of a maximum speed of 161 mph, the 944 Turbo accelerates from standstill to 62.5 mph in a mere 5.9 seconds. But of equal significance to the performance driver is the power spread over the rev range. Once again the 944 Turbo is impressive with over 250 Nm or 70% of the maximum torque being available from only 2,000 rpm through to 6,500 rpm, providing the driver with immediate acceleration at all times.

As would be expected from Porsche, such performance has not been achieved to the detriment of durability, efficiency, refinement or indeed, the environment. The 944 Turbo has a highly advanced engine management system (DME – Digital Motor Electronics), that calculates up to 400 times a second the optimum fuel/air mixture and ignition timing for maximum engine efficiency and performance.

Equally, twin contra-rotating balancer shafts spin at twice the engine speed thereby eliminating vibration and endowing the Porsche 4-cylinder engine with a characteristic smoothness and balance.

In addition, the 944 Turbo engine is fitted with a 'knock' sensor to automatically retard the electronic ignition or adjust the turbo boost-pressure, in order to alleviate any engine 'knock' during adverse conditions and so ensure consistent engine operation and maximum efficiency.

Finally, the 944 Turbo engine is both economical and environmentally responsible. Every new Porsche is now offered with a controlled 3-way exhaust gas catalytic converter to minimise environmentally harmful emissions, and operates on unleaded fuel without any loss of engine power or performance.

Water-cooled turbocharger with intercooler system for unrivalled performance.

Light aluminium alloy pistons and cylinder block.

Impressive torque available the rev range with over 250 2,000 and 6,500 rpm.

3 YEARS GUARANTEE

2-year mechanical, 3-year paint and 10-year anti-corrosion warranties

944 TURBO: RACE PROVEN PORSCHE TECHNOLOGY

It is fitting that the flagship of the 944 Series should owe its development to motorsport. In fact, the 944 Turbo engine and chassis are virtually identical to the cars that have competed for the past three seasons in the 944 Turbo Cup, the highly competitive European racing series.

Like its racing equivalent, the 944 Turbo has a 250 bhp engine that provides exhilarating acceleration without compromising long-term reliability. The car's competition heritage also ensures that the handling is both precise and responsive.

The 944 Turbo is a masterpiece of advanced automotive engineering not only in terms of performance technology but also optimised aerodynamic design.

The 944 Turbo incorporates 'ground-effect' technology whereby smooth underbody panels, together with the rear underbody spoiler, control the air passing underneath the car to create downforce and so increase high speed stability. In addition, the rear underbody spoiler encourages cooling air to circulate around the gearbox and exhaust system.

At the front, a deep polyurethane nose section, incorporating fog lights and auxiliary driving lamps, contributes to an excellent drag-coefficient of 0.33 but not at the expense of cross-wind instability or interior heat build-up.

Purpose-designed central air intakes ensure the optimum air flow to the engine intercooler and oil cooler as well as forced-air cooling to the front brakes.

Finally, the 944 Turbo is equipped with a new rear spoiler designed to reduce lift and therefore increase adhesion. This new spoiler completes the aerodynamic package and gives the 944 Turbo a unique identity to complement its outstanding performance.

The new rear spoiler reduces rear-end lift

The polyurethane shock absorbing bumpers help to provide impact protection at normal parking speeds

The 944 Series comes equipped with fog and auxiliary driving lights.

The powerful washer jet system keeps the head-lamps clear of road dirt.

FAR RIGHT, 1985: *Externally, the nose section was reprofiled into a one-piece bumper/spoiler unit with wider cooling slots and combined auxiliary driving and fog lights with wide slim indicators recessed above them. A body-colour rubbing strip was also added to the doors at waist height to protect the paintwork in car parks. At the rear, a new body pan and underbumper valence assisted the aerodynamics along with a larger spoiler at the base of the rear window. This helped to reduce the cd factor to 0.33 for the Turbo.*

ABOVE LEFT AND RIGHT, 1984–86: *The first performance upgrade to the 944 series came in 1985, courtesy of a turbocharger. This, together with some minor improvements, raised output by nearly 50 per cent to 217bhp, resulting in a top speed of just over 150mph (242kph).*

LEFT, 1985: *This model also received new 'telephone-dial' alloy wheels, similar to those fitted on the 928, but an inch wider than the standard 944 to accommodate fatter tyres. The usual suspension tuning assisted by four piston brake calipers ensured that chassis performance matched the considerable extra urge.*

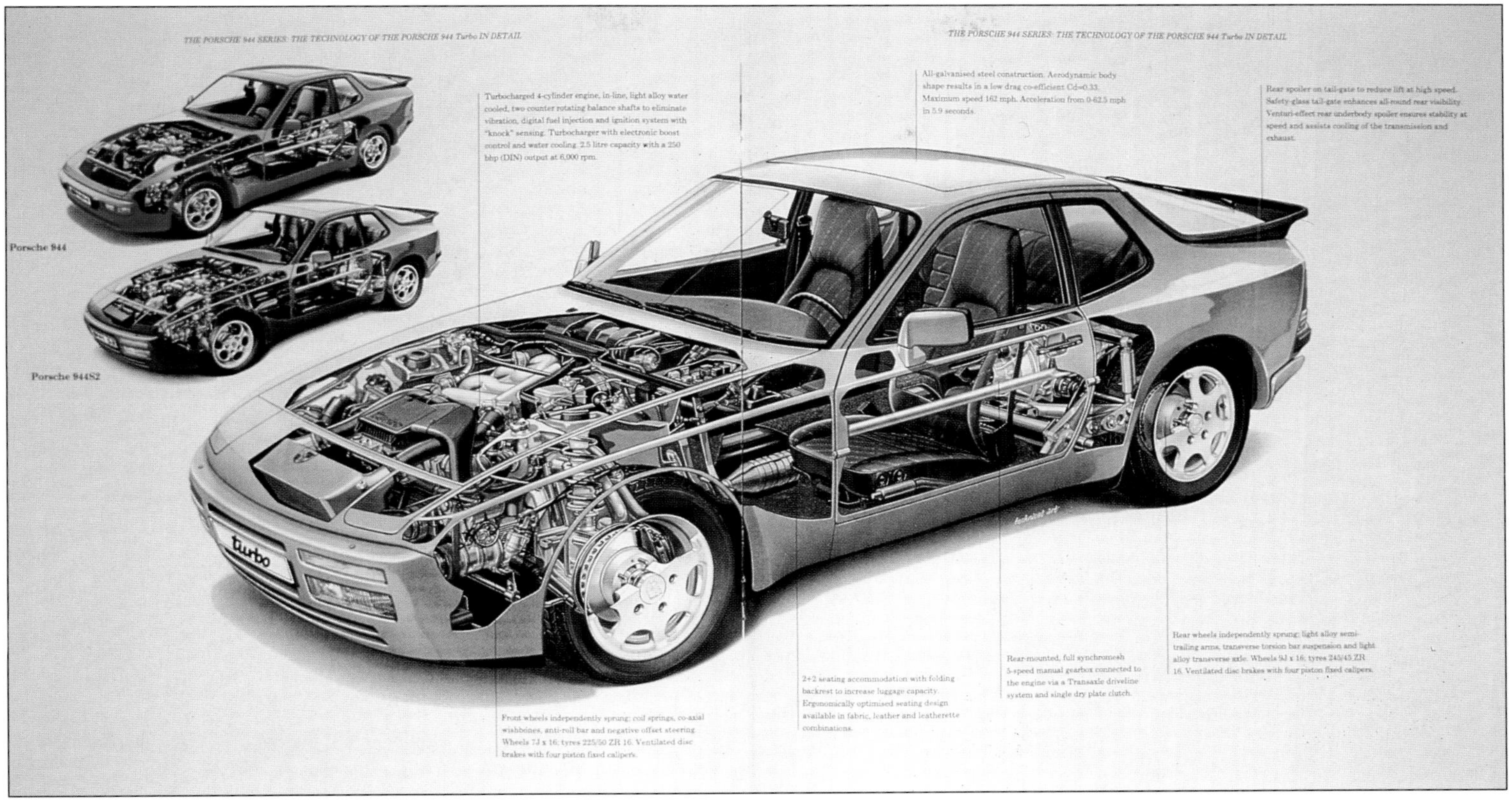

THE PORSCHE 944 SERIES: THE TECHNOLOGY OF THE PORSCHE 944 Turbo IN DETAIL

Porsche 944

Porsche 944S2

Turbocharged 4-cylinder engine, in-line, light alloy water cooled, two counter rotating balance shafts to eliminate vibration, digital fuel injection and ignition system with "knock" sensing. Turbocharger with electronic boost control and water cooling. 2.5 litre capacity with a 250 bhp (DIN) output at 6,000 rpm.

THE PORSCHE 944 SERIES: THE TECHNOLOGY OF THE PORSCHE 944 Turbo IN DETAIL

All-galvanised steel construction. Aerodynamic body shape results in a low drag co-efficient Cd=0.33. Maximum speed 162 mph. Acceleration from 0-62.5 mph in 5.9 seconds.

Rear spoiler on tail-gate to reduce lift at high speed. Safety-glass tail-gate enhances all-round rear visibility. Venturi-effect rear underbody spoiler ensures stability at speed and assists cooling of the transmission and exhaust.

Front wheels independently sprung; coil springs, co-axial wishbones, anti-roll bar and negative offset steering. Wheels 7J x 16; tyres 225/50 ZR 16. Ventilated disc brakes with four piston fixed callipers.

2+2 seating accommodation with folding backrest to increase luggage capacity. Ergonomically optimised seating design available in fabric, leather and leatherette combinations.

Rear-mounted, full synchromesh 5-speed manual gearbox connected to the engine via a Transaxle driveline system and single dry plate clutch.

Rear wheels independently sprung; light alloy semi-trailing arms, transverse torsion bar suspension and light alloy transverse axle. Wheels 9J x 16; tyres 245/45 ZR 16. Ventilated disc brakes with four piston fixed calipers.

LEFT, 1985: *Annual improvements have gradually increased the Turbo's performance, and although capacity remains at 2.5 litres, output on the latest models is 250bhp giving a top speed of 161mph (260kph) and 0–60mph acceleration time of under 6 seconds, well into 911 territory. The cars now sport Carrera 2-type alloy wheels and a further-revised rear spoiler similar in concept to the 959. Otherwise they are externally unchanged.*

RIGHT AND BELOW, 1987: *The introduction of the Turbo in 1986 produced a large performance, and price, gap between the two 944 models and this was filled a year later by an intermediate model called the 944S. This also used the 2.5-litre engine, but was fitted with a new cylinder head equipped with four valves per cylinder, and topped by twin overhead camshafts. This variant produced 188bhp, a top speed of 142mph (230kph) and 0–60mph acceleration time around 7 seconds, and fitted neatly between the other two models.*

THE PORSCHE 2.5 LITRE FAMILY: DESIGN PHILOSOPHY

AERODYNAMICS AND ROAD BEHAVIOUR

Today's 2.5 litre family of thoroughbred performance cars is a testimony to Porsche's renowned expertise and dedicated commitment to motorsport and research and development. Sleek, energy efficient body contours characterise each model's individualistic style.

This style and the timeless elegance of each model, combined with the highest standards of design, build quality, safety and performance, together with extensive warranties, ensures the long-term desirability of each model - each a true Porsche product with a distinctive performance and specification.

The futuristic body styling of each 2.5 litre model is not merely for the sake of appearance and long-term desirability. Their styling considerably influences fuel consumption, road performance and balanced handling. Effective aerodynamic styling of each model was a pre-requisite at the design stage. Extensive wind tunnel research minimised wind resistance, maximised air flow and indicated air pressure zones on the bodywork, so as to locate the "aerodynamic pressure point" in optimum relation to the vehicle's centre of gravity.

The resulting road behaviour has also been attained by reducing air-lift forces, thus dramatically improving straight-line running at speed and benefitting road holding and handling when braking and cornering. All models have a deep front spoiler to reduce underbody air turbulence and a rear spoiler to minimise air-lift forces. This also improves tyre adhesion and directional stability.

Equally, engine cooling and passenger compartment ventilation inlet positioning has been optimised in a wind tunnel, as have rain water channels, rubber door and window seals, mirrors and windscreen wipers.

Utilising Porsche's advanced 2.5 litre power unit, now developing 160 bhp (DIN), the 944 provides the exciting alternative to the Porsche 924 S. The Porsche 944 differs in both exterior and interior specification. Distinctive, wider, aerodynamic body contours provide the clearest example of how the Porsche 924 2+2 coupé concept has evolved.

The 944 achieves a maximum speed of over 135 mph, whilst maintaining outstanding fuel efficiency. These factors enabled the 944 to emerge as the most desired performance car in Britain, according to a recent major Automobile Association survey.

The 944 S is Porsche's latest contender for genuine supercar status. With a startling 16-valve cylinder head engine, developing 190 bhp (DIN), the 944 S offers even greater all-round performance. The significantly increased mid-range torque enables even greater acceleration and the maximum speed capability of 142 mph offers more enjoyment for the performance-minded driver.

LEFT, 1987: *Driving impressions of the 944 models have always been good. The balanced weight distribution and suspension design make it one of the better handling sports cars in the world, and the impression all three models give is that it would be difficult to find the limit of adhesion except by driving totally foolishly, in which case no designer, however brilliant, could save you anyway. The power steering gives just the right amount of assistance whilst maintaining feedback from the suspension. The basic 944 offered good performance and torque, and was probably the easiest to drive for the average enthusiast. The 944S demanded more urge to really exploit its performance, but this is a characteristic common to most 16-valve designs. The Turbo is a high-performance vehicle par excellence, and will reward the out-and-out enthusiast in a way few other cars can, especially in its price range.*

PORSCHE

FAR LEFT, 1989: *For 1989, the 944 range was reduced to just two models, at the top the Turbo, and below it a new model called the 944S2. This featured a 3-litre version of the 16-valve engine producing 211bhp, not far short of the original Turbo's output. This engine, currently the largest 4-cylinder unit in a production car, features a new cylinder block, lighter in weight than the previous unit. To further reduce weight, a plastic oil sump is used for the first time in any production car.*

LEFT, 1989: *Externally, the 944S2 is virtually identical to the Turbo model, the only distinguishing feature being the badging on the boot lid. Standard specification includes electric windows, central locking with combined alarm system, electrically adjustable seats, tinted, heat-filter glass all round and a centralized monitoring system for all the car's primary functions.*

LEFT, 1989: *Underneath the skin, the specification is just as impressive. ABS brakes are now standard, with ventilated discs all round. Suspension settings and tyre sizes are now the same as the original Turbo, and need to be as the performance is almost identical to that model with a top speed of 149mph (243kph). Torque, as one might expect, is plentiful making the 944S2 far more drivable than the original Turbo. The latest Bosch DME engine management system is fitted, and a 3-way exhaust catalytic convertor is standard.*

RIGHT, 1990: *1990 brought the introduction of the first body variant to the 944, a cabriolet. Available only to 944S2 specification, the Cabriolet features a completely restyled rear end with a fairly flat boot profile. The electrically-operated hood folds down into the rear deck and is protected by a fabric cover. The design retains the two occasional rear seats.*

THE NEW PORSCHE 944 SERIES: DEVELOPMENT PHILOSOPHY

The 'S2' also benefits from the bodyshell of the even more powerful 944 Turbo. This is not for the sake of appearance but for the sake of quite remarkable roadholding. "Ground-effect" technology helps give the 944S2 tremendous grip and sure-footed, high speed handling. Rare are the cars that put so much power at your fingertips. Rarer still are the cars with the means to exploit it to the full.

944S2 CABRIOLET - THE EXHILARATION OF FREEDOM

The 944S2 Cabriolet combines the razor-sharp performance of the Coupé model with all the sensual delights of soft-top motoring. Sleek, chic and sensationally fast, it is a compliment to the design philosophy behind the acclaimed Cabriolet concept so successful with the 911 Series.

Drivers of the 911 Cabriolet already appreciate the exhilaration of performance motoring "al-fresco". This experience is now available for those who appreciate the new performance potential and advanced exterior design of the 944S2.

The 'S2' body with its rigid Transaxle driveline is ideally suited for the conversion to a Cabriolet. Extra strengthening (the 'S2' has in effect two floor pans welded together) makes this a taut, reassuringly solid sports machine in the best traditions of Porsche. Equally sturdy is the Cabriolet hood. Double-lined and electrically-controlled (the only manual operation required is to release or lock the retaining catches), it keeps wind-noise to a minimum and is usable in all weather conditions. When down, a neat cover protects the hood from damage.

Other exclusive features on the 944S2 Cabriolet include a lower windscreen and a rear boot for generous luggage stowage. The rear seats also fold down to provide a practical through-loading facility. The 944S2 Cabriolet is one of most stylish convertibles in the world with performance equal to that of its Coupé counterpart.

Pictures: The new 94482 Cabriolet retains the Coupé lines and benefits from the aerodynamic enhancements applied to the 944 Turbo.

ABOVE, 1990: *With the hood down, the Cabriolet has a rakish profile and a much lower look than the coupe. When closed it has similarities to the early 356 Speedsters, the raised hood giving it a somewhat claustrophobic feel and, to some eyes, a clumsy unflattering profile. Pricewise, it fits neatly between the two coupe models. However, all new 944 prices are now quite high relative to the levels at which they were pitched on introduction. While most pundits have bemoaned the demise of a brand new 'entry-level' model, the combination of continued sales success and the stability of styling given by the evolutionary approach to upgrading the cars has brought a curious benefit to Porsche in the increased demand for second-hand versions mentioned earlier.*

928

As early as 1971, Porsche had started to look at a future replacement for the 911. As history now tells this was somewhat unnecessary, but at that time it would have been a brave man who would have forecast that the 911 would still be in serious production 20 years later. This would be the first Porsche to be designed from the ground up to an internal specification, the 356, 914 and 924 all having originated around Volkswagen parts, and the 911 being derived from the 356. The 928 arrived, somewhat unusually for Porsche, at the Geneva Motor Show in the spring of 1977. Its styling was striking, being the brain-child of Porsche's Design Chief at the time, an American called Tony Lapine. It was also a fairly large car, with a luxuriously appointed interior giving genuine 2+2 seating capacity. This was not a new sports car, more a Grand Tourer, and as such introduced Porsche to an entirely new market sector, at the time the almost exclusive territory of BMW and Mercedes Benz.

The basic concept for the new car was devised and agreed within a few days. It would be front-engined and have rear-wheel drive. To obtain as near optimum 50/50 weight distribution as possible, the gearbox would be rear-mounted in unit with the final drive. Because it was feared at the time that emission regulations would literally legislate air-cooled engines out of existence, the engine would have to be a new water-cooled unit. A V6 engine was initially considered, but ultimately rejected in favour of a V8. This would be fairly large capacity, which would make it acceptable to the American market.

The final crunch choice whether to go ahead with production of the car was made in 1973, against the background of soaring oil prices brought about by the Middle East situation. The go-ahead was given, a very brave decision at the time which could easily have backfired. Porsche's headaches were not over, however. Shortly after work commenced, the EA425 project was dropped by Volkswagen and another difficult choice had to be made. Should Porsche continue where VW left off, and if they did could both the internally and externally developed cars be pursued at the same time? Again the decision was positive and EA425 went on to become the 924 and the internal project became the 928.

The styling bore some resemblance to the 924, but was distinctive in its own right. The headlights were pop-up units, but laid-back into the front wings when retracted in a similar style to the Lamborghini Miura. There were also no separate bumpers as such, instead large deformable body-colour panels were fitted at the front and rear. The rear panel also housed the rear lights, and in the front panel, large units contained indicator, fog and driving lights.

BELOW, 1977–81: *Front suspension was a fairly conventional coil/ wishbone set-up, but the rear had a new design unique to the 928, and christened the 'Weissach Axle' in honour of the engineers at the Weissach Research and Development Centre who developed it. The design incorporated geometry aspects which counteracted oversteer in the event of deceleration during cornering.*

ABOVE, 1977–81: *The capacity of the new V8 engine was 4.5 litres with engine block and heads cast in alloy. A single belt-driven overhead camshaft operated on each bank of cylinders, and Bosch K-Jetronic fuel injection system was used. The engine developed 240bhp, giving a top speed of 144mph (233kph), and 0–60mph acceleration in the mid 7-second bracket. A five-speed gearbox was fitted, with a three-speed automatic option offered.*

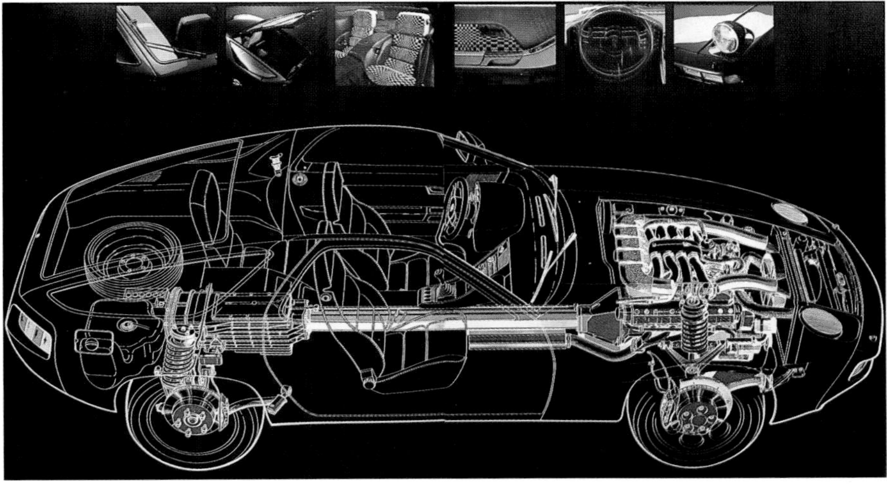

LEFT, 1977–81: *The suspension, combined with the almost perfect 51/49 per cent front/rear weight distribution produced vice-free neutral handling along with a supple ride. Testers waxed lyrical about the car's ride and performance, although some were critical about the roar generated by the wide, low-profile tyres.*

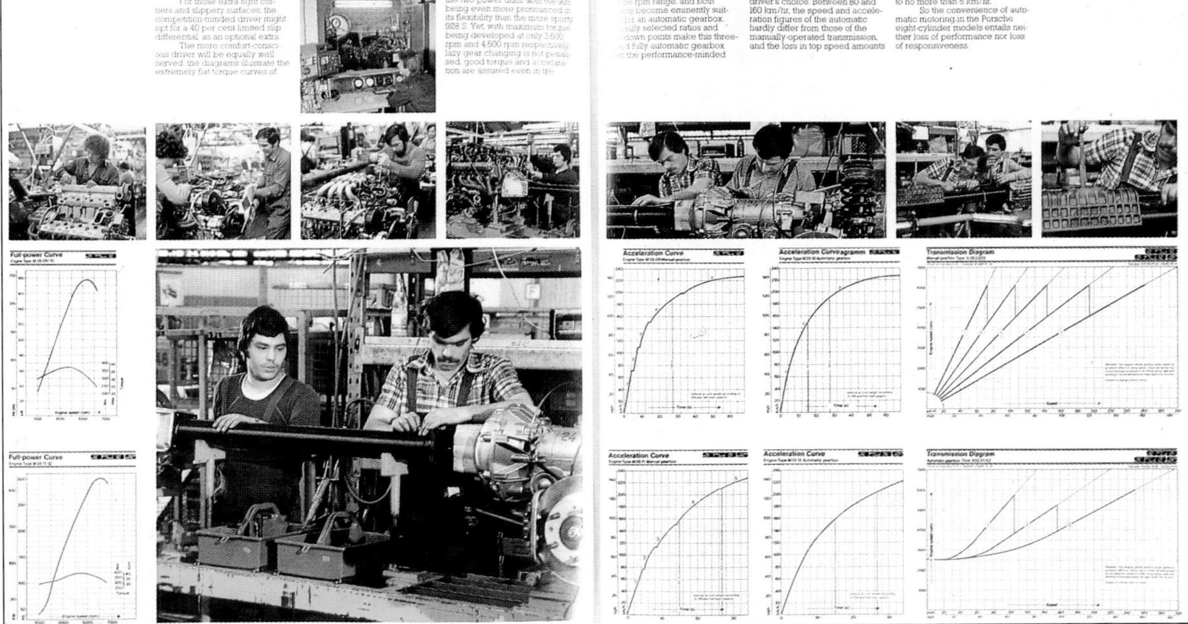

For those extra tight corners and slippery surfaces, the competition-minded driver might opt for a 40 per cent limited slip differential, as an optional extra.

The more comfort-conscious driver will be equally well served: the diagrams illustrate the extremely flat torque curves of the two power units, with the 928 being even more pronounced in its flexibility than the more sporty 928 S. Yet, with maximum torque being developed at only 3,600 rpm and 4,500 rpm respectively, lazy gear changing is not penalised, good torque and acceleration are assured even in the

rpm range, and both become eminently suit- for an automatic gearbox. selected ratios and down points make this three- fully automatic gearbox the performance-minded driver's choice. Between 80 and 160 km/hr, the speed and acceleration figures of the automatic hardly differ from those of the manually-operated transmission, and the loss in top speed amounts to no more than 5 km/hr.

So the convenience of automatic motoring in the Porsche eight-cylinder models entails neither loss of performance nor loss of responsiveness.

BELOW LEFT, 1979: *The large ventilated disc brakes all round also provided spectacular braking performance, stopping this quite heavy car in just 139 feet from 60mph. Some critics were not so happy with the interior of the car though. True it was the most opulent yet, and boasted a tilt-adjustable steering column (which also moved the instrument panel to maintain good visibility of the gauges for the driver), power windows, cruise control, central locking, rear seat sunvisors and an air conditioning system that even cooled the glovebox. It was the awful op-art cloth upholstery which was disliked, although leather was an option, and soon became standard to resolve the problem.*

Porsche 928:
Sports Car without Space Problems.

Superb space engineering in the Porsche 928 made it possible to provide seating for two adults in front and two children or teenagers in back. There is also a spacious cargo area for their belongings. Altogether, an unusual feat in a pure sports car.

A spare tire is stowed out of the way beneath the rear deck. With it are the electric inflation pump, tire-changing tools, and the battery. The added weight of these items in the rear provides optimum weight distribution and serves as a counter-balance for the power train. A complete tool kit is also furnished in a fitted case across the back of the trunk area.

Ideal access to the trunk space is provided through an ample rear hatch opening. The entire hatch unit, including the rear window, is lifted and held open by gas-filled struts. It opens on a wide, carpeted cargo area, with a net at the forward end to help prevent items from moving forward in fast stops. A special cover (standard equipment) conceals the contents of the cargo bay from prying eyes.

The storage area can be greatly enlarged by simply folding down the backs of one or both rear seats. This design flexibility takes full advantage of the spaciousness Porsche has engineered into the 928.

A number of storage compartments are provided throughout the 928 for small items. In front, there is a deep, lockable glove compartment. In each door, there is a spacious bin for maps and other travel needs. For security, a knob is provided at the rear of each door for retracting the lock button, making it all but impossible to lift them from outside of the car. For even greater security, an optional anti-theft system is available for the 928.

Specifications, standard equipment and options subject to change without prior notice.

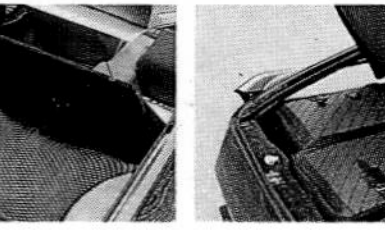

LEFT AND BELOW, 1980: *The first development of the new car came in 1979 with the introduction of the 928S. Engine capacity was increased to 4.7 litres producing around 280bhp. This gave a top speed of 155mph (250kph), 0–60mph acceleration of just over 6 seconds, and 0–100mph in just 14.6 seconds.*

LEFT, 1983: *Porsche management had expected most of the 928's sales to come from what are known as conquests, ie winning-over a customer from a rival make, rather than its existing owners moving-up. At first, however, nearly 40 per cent of 928 buyers were existing Porsche owners expecting it to be the same as their last car, but more so. Although nearly all of the new recruits were delighted with the car, the old school were mainly disappointed because the 928 was different, was intended to be different, and would continue to develop its own character. In 1984, the 928S2 arrived with further engine modifications raising output to nearly 300bhp, and producing a top speed of 158mph (254kph). ABS braking became standard, as did electrically-operated front seats. 1987 brought the first major revision with the introduction 928S4.*

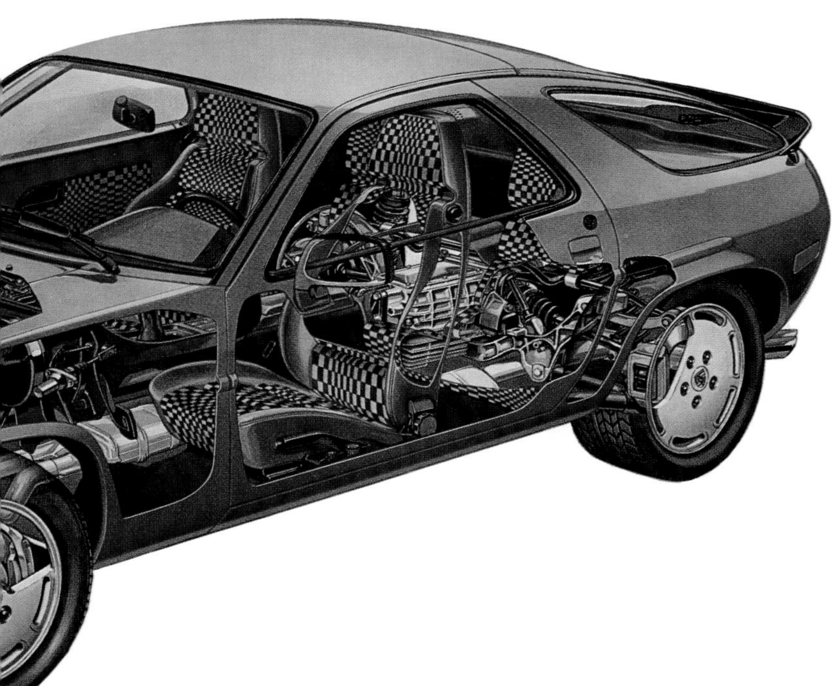

LEFT, 1980: *Externally, the car sprouted fairly innocuous aerodynamic aids, a small chin spoiler under the front panel, and a rear spoiler at the base of the rear window. New and distinctive eight-spoke alloy wheels were fitted to the 928S to distinguish it from the 'ordinary' 928 which retained the 'telephone-dial' type.*

ABOVE, 1987: *1987 brought the first major revision with the introduction of the 928S4. This model boasts a 5-litre engine with four valves per cylinder operated by twin overhead camshafts on each bank of cylinders. A four-speed automatic transmission was made standard, with the five-speed manual gearbox being offered as a no-cost option, a further demonstration of the different type of owner that the 928 was attracting.*

ABOVE, 1990: *A four-seater has been made as a special one-off for Ferry Porsche, and Ernst Fuhrmann has received a turbocharged variant. The engine could be increased in capacity to 5.5 litres with little modification, so there is probably a good ten years of life left in the 928, maybe more.*

BELOW, 1987: *Externally, the nose section has been redesigned and is now more rounded in shape reminiscent of the 944 Turbo. The rear panel has also been redesigned and incorporates larger wrap-around tail light units. A new and larger spoiler stands proud of the tailgate at the rear.*

ABOVE, 1987: *Power output for the new engine is 320bhp, producing a top speed of 165mph (267kph). In 1989, the manual gearbox option was dropped on the S4, but one development was still to come which would prove to be the ultimate derivative of this car, thus far.*

DRIVER SAFETY: PORSCHE'S PRIMARY CONSIDERATION

To enable the sporting driver to enjoy the full performance potential of the 928 Series, there has been a strong design commitment to driving safety.

The 928 is not only one of the fastest but also the safest cars in the world. Both the 928 S4 and 928 GT have large reserves of engine power allowing the driver to respond quickly to any given situation. A powerful anti-lock braking system is also featured to provide the stopping power equal to this performance potential.

In addition to these active safety features, the 928 Series also incorporates many passive safety features to protect the occupants in the event of an accident.

The polyurethane body panels at the front and rear, encasing high strength shock absorbing bumpers, are deformable to minimise damage in the case of an impact at normal parking speeds.

Also, unusually large front and rear deformation zones are a feature of the design in order to absorb impact energy in a collision. [illegible]mental to the Transaxle driveline which connects the front mounted engine to the rear mounted gearbox, literally forming the backbone of the car and achieving near-perfect weight distribution.

In the event of an accident, this strengthened steel driveline has the advantage of passing the force of the impact from the front to the rear of the car, or vice versa, so bypassing the occupants.

The exceptionally strong roof, windscreen pillars and door frames, equipped with side-intrusion bars, combine to create an effective roll-over cage.

Coupled with the deformation zones, this forms a "safety cell" to protect the occupants of the car. Safety locks prevent the doors opening during an accident yet the rigid construction helps to ensure against the doors jamming.

Finally, the petrol tank and fuel pipes are designed to help to prevent fuel escape following impact damage.

Inside the car many other safety measures have been taken. The interior is padded with [illegible]sorbing flame retardant materials in all critical areas, whilst the deformable instrument panel has a splinter-proof frame extending into the footwells. For added driving safety, the cushioned steering wheel is collapsible to protect the driver and the windscreen is laminated to help prevent shattering.

Unrivalled build quality is supported by a 10-year anti-corrosion warranty.

The polyurethane rear section encases shock absorbing bumpers.

The wind-tunnel developed rear spoiler smooths the airflow for maximum stability and reduced lift.

The rear wiper ensures optimum visibility at all times.

The 928 is equipped with recessed front and rear lamp clusters.

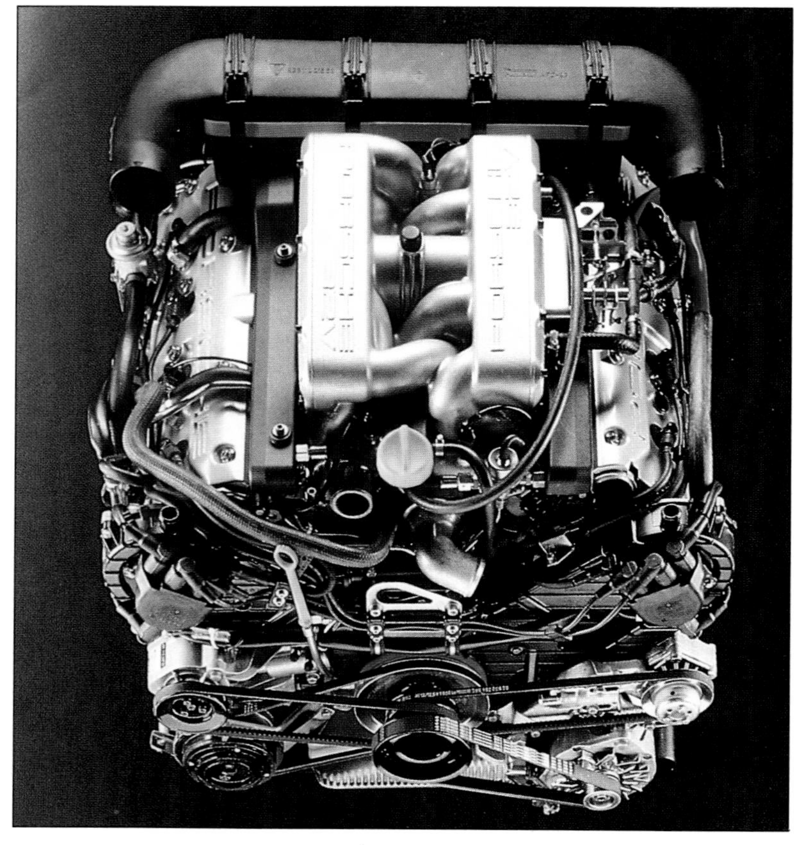

ABOVE LEFT AND LEFT, 1990: *The 928GT was introduced at the beginning of 1990 and standard equipment includes electronic variable limited-slip differential, and a sophisticated on-board computer called the 'Porsche Information and Diagnostic System' which monitors all the car's main functions and safety factors, even warning the driver of low tyre pressures.*

ABOVE, 1990: *It features the most powerful, 330bhp, variant of the 5-litre engine. Available only with a five-speed manual gearbox, the 928GT will reach a top speed of 171mph (277kph), and accelerate from 0–60mph in just 5.6 seconds.*

928 GT: THE PINNACLE OF SPORTING PERFORMANCE

The more sporting character of the 928 GT results from specific developments to the powerful 5-litre, 8-cylinder engine.

These modifications raise engine output to a formidable 330 bhp DIN (243 kW) at 6,200 rpm. Sharing the same muscular torque as the 928 S4, the 928 GT also produces 430 Nm but at a higher, more vigorous 4,100 rpm.

With the increased engine power combined with the lower rear axle drive ratio, mid-range and top-end performance are even more sensational, allowing the 928 GT to respond instantly to every driver command.

These dynamic enhancements have been achieved through the installation of a modified engine management system and a fine tuned air intake system. Uprated camshafts with revised valve timing have also been fitted, whilst the rev limiter has been raised to 6,800 rpm.

The light twin tail exhaust system allows the driver to hear as well as feel the difference of the 928 GT. Even so, the engine remains surprisingly quiet even at high speed.

The 928 Series features a unique air intake system to ensure optimised engine performance. This advanced system automatically adjusts the air inlets in the nose section to ensure maximum engine cooling during high thermal loads, in accordance with aerodynamic efficiency.

Three-stage movable inlet flaps, located in front of the radiator, and two variable electric fans situated behind the radiator regulate the rate of airflow.

These electrically adjustable flaps will only allow sufficient air into the engine compartment as is needed for maximum engine efficiency and air conditioning requirements.

When thermal loads are reduced, this automatic regulation closes the inlets, ensuring optimised engine temperature for efficiency and fuel economy, as well as aerodynamic effectiveness.

The 928 GT is a remarkable car even by Porsche standards and represents the Porsche definition of a true 'Gran Turismo'.

32

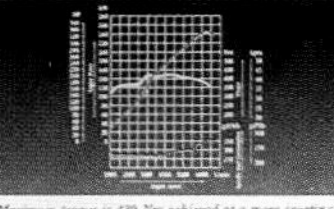

Performance modifications to the 5-litre V8 engine include a revised engine management system, raising the maximum power to 330 bhp (DIN).

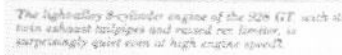

Maximum torque is 430 Nm achieved at a more sporting 4,100 rpm allowing the 928 GT to accelerate from 0-62.5 mph in 5.8 seconds.

The lightalloy 8-cylinder engine of the 928 GT, with its twin exhaust tailpipes and raised rev limiter, is surprisingly quiet even at high engine speed.

33

ABOVE AND RIGHT, 1990: *With Porsche's known policy of continual development, it is doubtful that we have yet seen the 'ultimate' 928. The styling is still fresh even after nearly 14 years, indeed this is what was intended at the outset.*

928 GT: THE PORSCHE SPORTING GRAN TURISMO

The 928 GT represents the ultimate reward for the high performance driver.

Adding a further dimension to the performance of the 928 Series, the 928 GT takes the 'Gran Turismo' concept into the highest realms of dynamic driving pleasure.

Providing pure exhilaration whilst losing none of the 928 S4's unique sophistication, the 928 GT is exclusively available with a 5-speed manual transmission, with a shorter final drive ratio to maximise the performance potential. A short Sport gearshift is also fitted to encourage superbly swift and precise gear changes, perfect for demanding cross-country motoring.

Whilst the 928 GT shares the same powerful 5-litre 32-valve V8 engine as the 928 S4, it is specifically uprated for even greater performance potential. Capable of 10 bhp more than the 928 S4, the 928 GT produces a massive 330 bhp (DIN) with enhanced all round responsiveness and surprising fuel economy.

With a top speed of over 170 mph, this modified engine powers the 928 GT from rest to 62.5 mph in only 5.8 seconds.

As with the 928 S4, the 928 GT is equipped with a controlled 3-way catalytic converter with no loss of performance. This converter is extremely efficient in removing environmentally harmful gases from the 928's exhaust emission.

To handle the increased power, the chassis of the 928 GT has been selectively modified from that of the 928 S4, reflecting Porsche's vast range of racing experience.

Changes to the suspension include stiffened adjustable gas-filled Sport shock absorbers and uprated springs. The rear track is widened by 17mm for impressive stability, whilst wider wheels add to the 928 GT's phenomenal road holding abilities.

Measuring 7.5J x 16 at the front and 9J x 16 at the rear, and fitted with 225/50 ZR 16 and 245/45 ZR 16 ultra low profile tyres respectively, the advanced pressure cast light alloy 'Design 90' wheels provide the 928 GT with a unique identity. These wheels feature enlarged openings which are designed to channel cooling air away from the immensely powerful disc brakes.

Naturally, in light of its sporting capabilities, the 928 GT is also equipped with the unique new PSD electronically controlled, variable transverse rear differential system.

These chassis and transmission enhancements ensure that the exceptional power of the 928 GT can be easily and effectively applied to the road.

Yet for all of its sporting performance, the 928 GT is no raw racer. Instead it shares the same sumptuous equipment of the 928 S4.

30

The 928 GT features a short gearshift for rapid and precise changes.

The 5-speed manual transmission has a shorter final drive ratio.

Pressure cast light alloy Design 90 wheels give the 928 GT a unique identity.

The coil springs, which enclose telescopic dampers, are height adjustable.

31

959

Porsche's latest offspring, first shown as a design study in 1981, received the designation 959 and became the first entrant in the new media category of 'Supercars', road-legal vehicles with a top speed in excess of 200mph (324kph), state-of-the-art design features and price tags to match. Even so, the initial price of around $250,000 (£135,000) guaranteed an immediate sell-out. Even by today's standards, this was an absolute bargain.

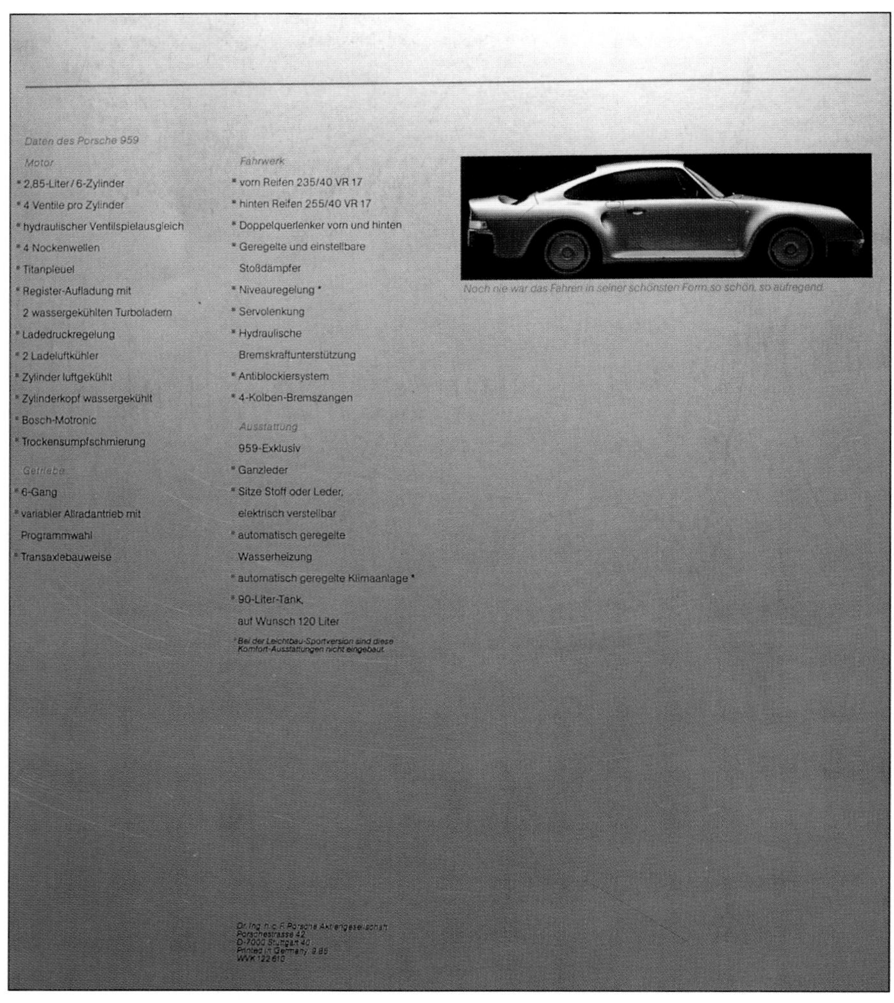

Daten des Porsche 959

Motor
* 2,85-Liter / 6-Zylinder
* 4 Ventile pro Zylinder
* hydraulischer Ventilspielausgleich
* 4 Nockenwellen
* Titanpleuel
* Register-Aufladung mit 2 wassergekühlten Turboladern
* Ladedruckregelung
* 2 Ladeluftkühler
* Zylinder luftgekühlt
* Zylinderkopf wassergekühlt
* Bosch-Motronic
* Trockensumpfschmierung

Getriebe
* 6-Gang
* variabler Allradantrieb mit Programmwahl
* Transaxlebauweise

Fahrwerk
* vorn Reifen 235/40 VR 17
* hinten Reifen 255/40 VR 17
* Doppelquerlenker vorn und hinten
* Geregelte und einstellbare Stoßdämpfer
* Niveauregelung *
* Servolenkung
* Hydraulische Bremskraftunterstützung
* Antiblockiersystem
* 4-Kolben-Bremszangen

Ausstattung

959-Exklusiv
* Ganzleder
* Sitze Stoff oder Leder, elektrisch verstellbar
* automatisch geregelte Wasserheizung
* automatisch geregelte Klimaanlage *
* 90-Liter-Tank, auf Wunsch 120 Liter

** Bei der Leichtbau-Sportversion sind diese Komfort-Ausstattungen nicht eingebaut.*

Noch nie war das Fahren in seiner schönsten Form so schön, so aufregend.

Dr. Ing. h.c. F. Porsche Aktiengesellschaft
Porschestrasse 42
D-7000 Stuttgart 40
Printed in Germany 9.85
WVK 122 610

At the Frankfurt Motor Show in 1981, Porsche showed a static design study based on the 911 which would be developed into a Group B rally car. In 1986 that project made its debut in the Paris-Dakar rally which it won. More successes followed and a limited production run of 250 cars was announced which would be available for sale as road cars to an exclusive and very lucky few.

The initial price also included a visit to the Nürburgring circuit in Germany for a factory-run familiarization course, because this is no ordinary vehicle. The engine is a special short-stroke 2.85-litre flat-6 cylinder unit. It has titanium rods and crankshaft and, as on the sports racing cars of recent years, the cylinder barrels are air-cooled whilst the heads are water-cooled. Each head houses four valves per cylinder operated by twin overhead camshafts. Twin KKK turbochargers boost maximum output to 450bhp produced at 6500rpm, with peak torque of 370lb/ft coming in at 5500rpm. All of this produces a top speed of 205mph (332kph) at 7500rpm and an acceleration time from 0–60mph of 3.9 seconds. The mere 12 cars allocated to the UK market were in fact pre-sold ahead of the official announcement, all to existing Porsche owners, and such has been the demand since in Britain alone that there are now nearly 50 examples residing there.

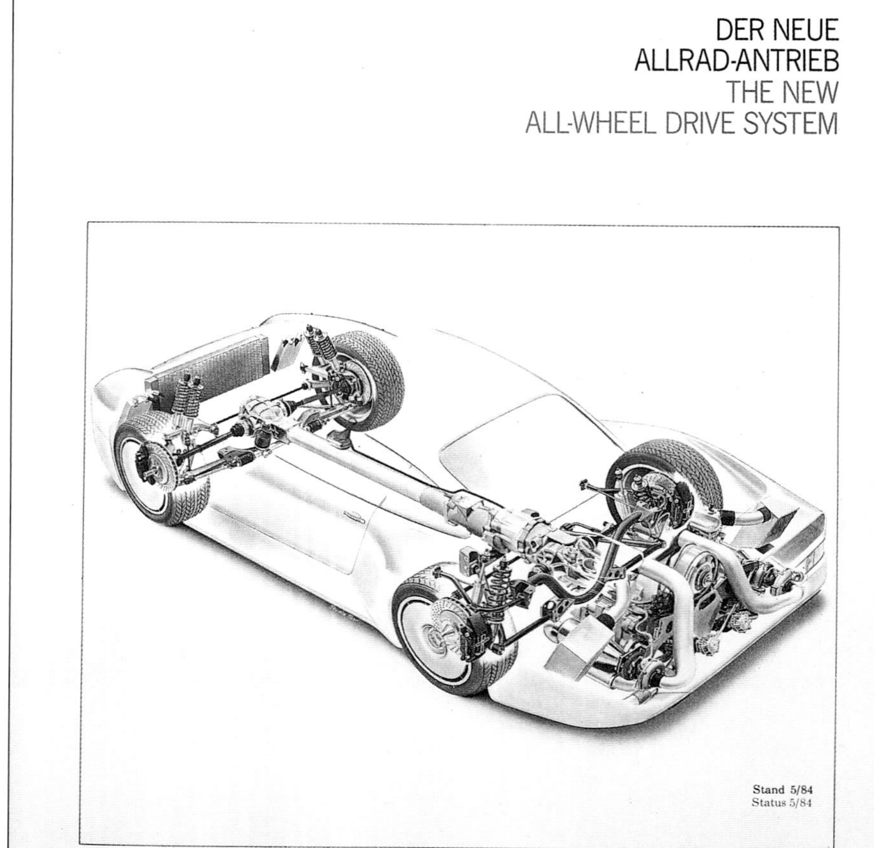

ABOVE, 1987: *Two versions of the car were built. The 'Comfort' model included air conditioning and additional sound insulation. The 'Sport' version omitted these, along with the rear seats and other such niceties to provide raw performance.*

BELOW, 1987: *An all-new four-wheel drive transmission was used, with a conventional mid-mounted six-speed gearbox connected to a front transaxle by a large tube housing the propshaft. The front differential casing also housed a torque-splitting clutch. Through the new computer control system electronic signals are generated by sensors giving engine speed, throttle position, and wheel speed. The latter is derived from the same sensors which control the ABS braking system.*

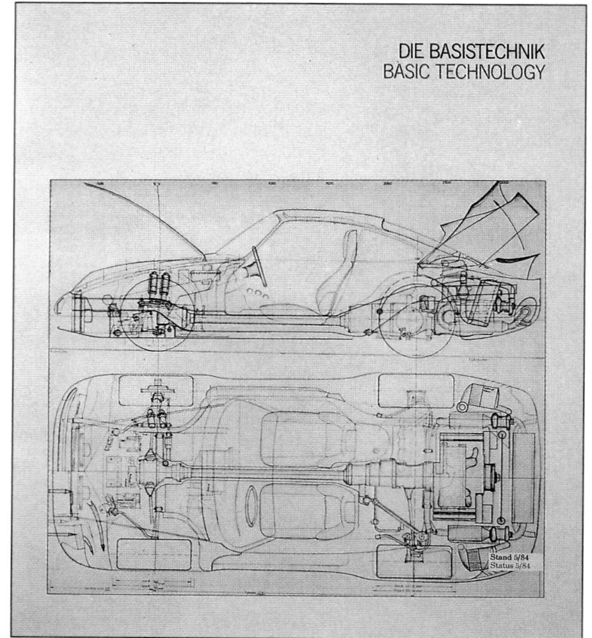

LEFT, 1987: *The computer can therefore calculate rate of acceleration, and thereby the weight transfer front-to-rear can be 'mapped'. With the rear wheels directly driven, the front axle torque can be varied by the computer to give the optimum traction. This can be controlled manually by the driver, or one of four pre-programmed schedules can be selected to assist with varying road conditions. The computer varies the rate of rear-to-front torque transfer in each mode and also monitors relative wheel speed thus predicting wheel spin which it counteracts by locking the appropriate clutch. The 'Dry' programme offers a variable front/rear split percentage between 40/60 and 20/80 depending on road conditions, the latter being selected for out-and-out acceleration. The 'Wet' setting fixes the split at 40/60. 'Ice' gives an even 50/50 split, and 'Traction' locks-up all clutches and differentials for maximum pulling power in off-road or snow conditions. Response time of the system is between 50 and 100 milliseconds.*

959 – Der neue Porsche Sportwagen

Die Idee kam vor wenigen Jahren: Das Porsche-Wissen in ein Auto hineinzustecken, die ganzen Erfahrungen mit erfolgreichen Sportwagen – vom 356 über den 911 bis zum 956 –, von den Gedanken des Prof. Porsche zum Allradantrieb über Meilensteine der Turbo-Aufladung bis hin zur Technik des Raumfahrt-Zeitalters, die zum Handwerkszeug des Entwicklungszentrums Weissach gehören.

Die Aufgabe

Der Porsche 959 – ein völlig neuer Sportwagen, faszinierend in Technik und Styling, entwickelt auf dem sicheren Fundament gründlicher Erfahrung und konzipiert als Schritt ins Zeitalter intelligenter Autos.

Das Ergebnis

Das Haus Porsche fertigt von dem straßenerprobten Zukunftssportwagen 959 zweihundert Fahrzeuge.

Der 959 ist ein exklusives Hochleistungsfahrzeug mit aufwendiger Technik.

Zahlreiche Elemente sind direkt aus der Renntechnik übernommen.

Beim 959 werden hochwertige Werkstoffe in der gediegenen Qualität verarbeitet, die in Zuffenhausen Standard ist.

Er ist alltagstauglich erprobt nach strengen Maßstäben.

Der Sportwagen 959 erschließt eine bisher nicht gekannte Klasse in Fahrleistung und klarem sicherem Fahrverhalten. Er ist zugeschnitten auf den engagierten und versierten Kenner, der bei der Weiterentwicklung des Sportwagens mitsprechen will.

Der Motor des 959 ist auf umweltfreundlichen bleifreien Kraftstoff (95 Oktan) abgestimmt. Auf Wunsch können auch Katalysatoren eingebaut werden.

LEFT, 1987: *The body is basically that of a 911 Turbo, with steel components galvanized and additional body panels manufactured from Kevlar and other GRP materials. The windscreen is bullet-proof. Braking is courtesy of large ventilated discs from a 956, servo-operated with full anti-lock capability, very necessary to stop this 28cwt projectile with a power-to-weight ratio of around 320bhp/ton, over four times that requested by Ferry Porsche when specifying the first 356 Carrera 30 years earlier. The suspension is a coil spring/double wishbone design very similar to a racing set-up. Concentric coil springs are used together with twin shock-absorbers on each wheel. Each shock-absorber has electronically-adjustable variable damping circuitry built in, allowing for computer-control which can vary not only the car's ride height, but also the angle of the body relative to the road. This further enhances the ground-effect generated by underbody airflow and adds yet more stability to the handling.*

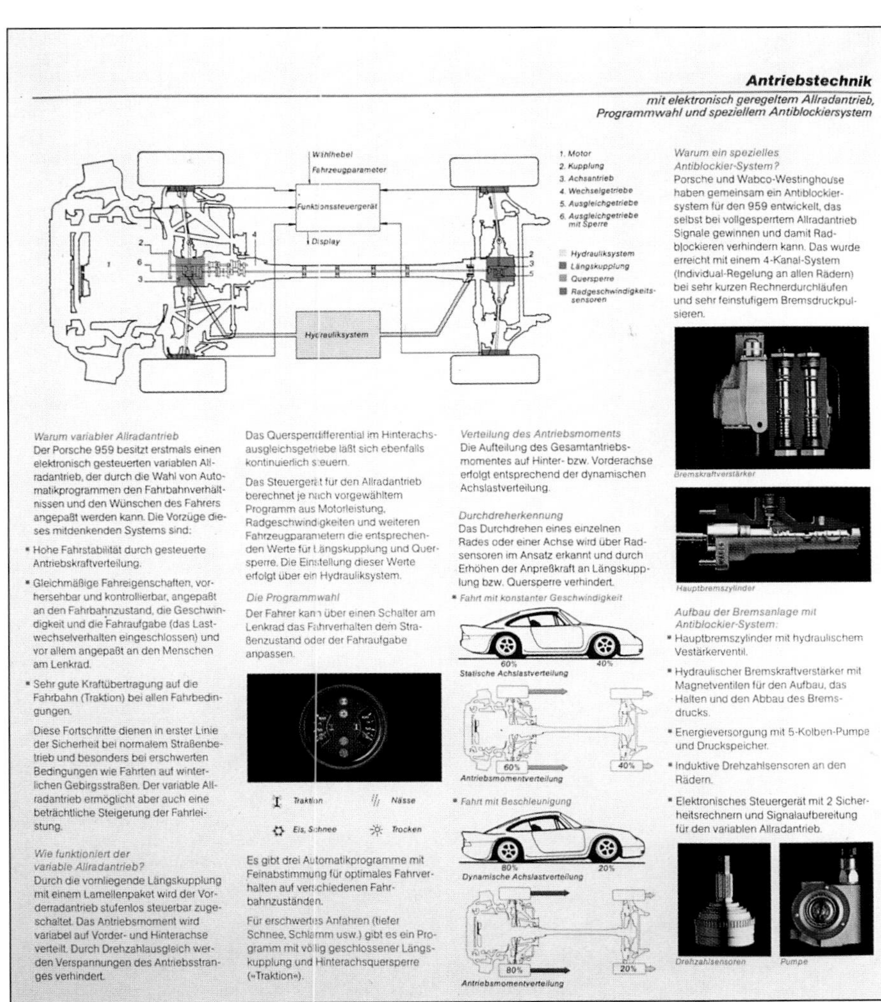

Antriebstechnik

mit elektronisch geregeltem Allradantrieb, Programmwahl und speziellem Antiblockiersystem

Wählhebel
Fahrzeugparameter
Funktionssteuergerät
Display
Hydrauliksystem

1. Motor
2. Kupplung
3. Achsantrieb
4. Wechselgetriebe
5. Ausgleichgetriebe
6. Ausgleichgetriebe mit Sperre

Hydrauliksystem
Längskupplung
Quersperre
Radgeschwindigkeitssensoren

Warum variabler Allradantrieb
Der Porsche 959 besitzt erstmals einen elektronisch gesteuerten variablen Allradantrieb, der durch die Wahl von Automatikprogrammen den Fahrbahnverhältnissen und den Wünschen des Fahrers angepaßt werden kann. Die Vorzüge dieses mitdenkenden Systems sind:

- Hohe Fahrstabilität durch gesteuerte Antriebskraftverteilung.
- Gleichmäßige Fahreigenschaften, vorhersehbar und kontrollierbar, angepaßt an den Fahrbahnzustand, die Geschwindigkeit und die Fahraufgabe (das Lastwechselverhalten eingeschlossen) und vor allem angepaßt an den Menschen am Lenkrad.
- Sehr gute Kraftübertragung auf die Fahrbahn (Traktion) bei allen Fahrbedingungen.

Diese Fortschritte dienen in erster Linie der Sicherheit bei normalem Straßenbetrieb und besonders bei erschwerten Bedingungen wie Fahrten auf winterlichen Gebirgsstraßen. Der variable Allradantrieb ermöglicht aber auch eine beträchtliche Steigerung der Fahrleistung.

Wie funktioniert der variable Allradantrieb?
Durch die vornliegende Längskupplung mit einem Lamellenpaket wird der Vorderradantrieb stufenlos steuerbar zugeschaltet. Das Antriebsmoment wird variabel auf Vorder- und Hinterachse verteilt. Durch Drehzahlausgleich werden Verspannungen des Antriebsstranges verhindert.

Das Querspenrdifferential im Hinterachsausgleichsgetriebe läßt sich ebenfalls kontinuierlich steuern.

Das Steuergerät für den Allradantrieb berechnet je nach vorgewähltem Programm aus Motorleistung, Radgeschwindigkeiten und weiteren Fahrzeugparametern die entsprechenden Werte für Längskupplung und Quersperre. Die Einstellung dieser Werte erfolgt über ein Hydrauliksystem.

Die Programmwahl
Der Fahrer kann über einen Schalter am Lenkrad das Fahrverhalten dem Straßenzustand oder der Fahraufgabe anpassen.

Traktion — Nässe — Eis, Schnee — Trocken

Es gibt drei Automatikprogramme mit Feinabstimmung für optimales Fahrverhalten auf verschiedenen Fahrbahnzuständen.

Für erschwertes Anfahren (tiefer Schnee, Schlamm usw.) gibt es ein Programm mit völlig geschlossener Längskupplung und Hinterachsquersperre (»Traktion«).

Verteilung des Antriebsmoments
Die Aufteilung des Gesamtantriebsmomentes auf Hinter- bzw. Vorderachse erfolgt entsprechend der dynamischen Achslastverteilung.

Durchdreherkennung
Das Durchdrehen eines einzelnen Rades oder einer Achse wird über Radsensoren im Ansatz erkannt und durch Erhöhen der Anpreßkraft an Längskupplung bzw. Quersperre verhindert.

- *Fahrt mit konstanter Geschwindigkeit*

60% 40%
Statische Achslastverteilung
60% 40%
Antriebsmomentverteilung

- *Fahrt mit Beschleunigung*

80% 20%
Dynamische Achslastverteilung
80% 20%
Antriebsmomentverteilung

Warum ein spezielles Antiblockier-System?
Porsche und Wabco-Westinghouse haben gemeinsam ein Antiblockiersystem für den 959 entwickelt, das selbst bei vollgesperrtem Allradantrieb Signale gewinnen und damit Radblockieren verhindern kann. Das wurde erreicht mit einem 4-Kanal-System (Individual-Regelung an allen Rädern) bei sehr kurzen Rechnerdurchläufen und sehr feinstufigem Bremsdruckpulsieren.

Bremskraftverstärker

Hauptbremszylinder

Aufbau der Bremsanlage mit Antiblockier-System:
- Hauptbremszylinder mit hydraulischem Vestärkerventil.
- Hydraulischer Bremskraftverstärker mit Magnetventilen für den Aufbau, das Halten und den Abbau des Bremsdrucks.
- Energieversorgung mit 5-Kolben-Pumpe und Druckspeicher.
- Induktive Drehzahlsensoren an den Rädern.
- Elektronisches Steuergerät mit 2 Sicherheitsrechnern und Signalaufbereitung für den variablen Allradantrieb.

Drehzahlsensoren — Pumpe

ABOVE, 1987: *The ride height is electronically adjustable between 120 and 180mm (4.5 and 7 inches). The lower setting is selected at speeds above 75mph and at this level the airflow produces zero-lift and a drag co-efficient of 0.31.*

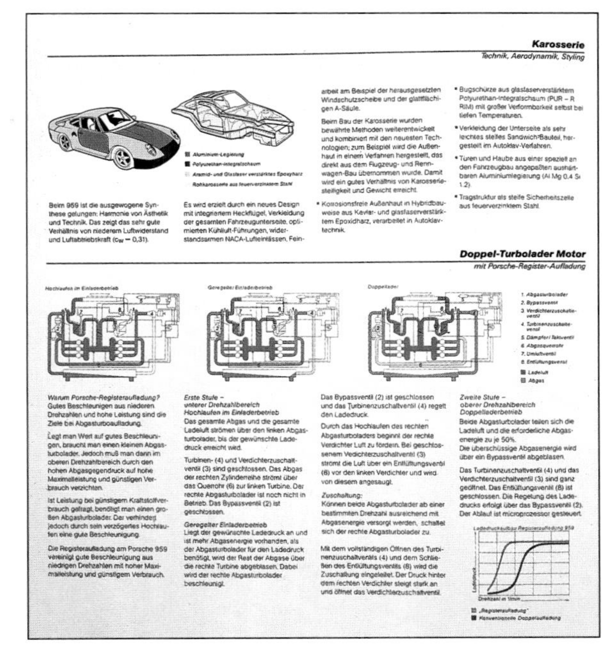

Karosserie

Technik, Aerodynamik, Styling

Aluminium-Legierung
Polyurethan-Integralschaum
Aramid- und Glasfaser verstärktes Epoxyharz
Rohkarosserie aus feuerverzinktem Stahl

Beim 959 ist die ausgewogene Synthese gelungen: Harmonie von Ästhetik und Technik. Das zeigt das sehr gute Verhältnis von niederem Luftwiderstand und Luftabtriebskraft (c_W – 0,31).

Es wird erzielt durch ein neues Design mit integriertem Heckflügel, Verkleidung der gesamten Fahrzeugunterseite, optimierten Kühlluft-Führungen, widerstandsarmen NACA-Lufteinlässen, Feinarbeit am Beispiel der herausgesetzten Windschutzscheibe und der glattflächigen A-Säule.

Beim Bau der Karosserie wurden bewährte Methoden weiterentwickelt und kombiniert mit den neuesten Technologien; zum Beispiel wird die Außenhaut in einem Verfahren hergestellt, das direkt aus dem Flugzeug- und Rennwagen-Bau übernommen wurde. Damit wird ein gutes Verhältnis von Karosseriesteifigkeit und Gewicht erreicht.

- Korrosionsfreie Außenhaut in Hybridbauweise aus Kevlar- und glasfaserverstärktem Epoxidharz, verarbeitet in Autoklavtechnik.
- Bugschürze aus glasfaserverstärktem Polyurethan-Integralschaum (PUR – R RIM) mit großer Verformbarkeit selbst bei tiefen Temperaturen.
- Verkleidung der Unterseite als sehr leichtes steifes Sandwich-Bauteil, hergestellt im Autoklav-Verfahren.
- Türen und Haube aus einer speziell an den Fahrzeugbau angepaßten aushärtbaren Aluminiumlegierung (Al Mg 0.4 Si 1.2).
- Tragstruktur als steife Sicherheitszelle aus feuerverzinktem Stahl.

Doppel-Turbolader Motor

mit Porsche-Register-Aufladung

Hochlaufen im Einladerbetrieb
Geregelter Einladerbetrieb
Doppellader

1. Abgasturbolader
2. Bypassventil
3. Verdichterzuschaltventil
4. Turbinenzuschaltventil
5. Dämpfer/Taktventil
6. Abgasquerrohr
7. Umluftventil
8. Entlüftungsventil

Ladeluft
Abgas

Warum Porsche-Registeraufladung?
Gutes Beschleunigen aus niederen Drehzahlen und hohe Leistung sind die Ziele bei Abgasturboaufladung.

Legt man Wert auf gutes Beschleunigen, braucht man einen kleinen Abgasturbolader. Jedoch muß man dann im oberen Drehzahlbereich durch den hohen Abgasgegendruck auf hohe Maximalleistung und günstigen Verbrauch verzichten.

Ist Leistung bei günstigem Kraftstoffverbrauch gefragt, benötigt man einen großen Abgasturbolader. Der verhindert jedoch durch sein verzögertes Hochlaufen eine gute Beschleunigung.

Die Registeraufladung am Porsche 959 vereinigt gute Beschleunigung aus niedrigen Drehzahlen mit hoher Maximalleistung und günstigem Verbrauch.

Erste Stufe – unterer Drehzahlbereich Hochlaufen im Einladerbetrieb
Das gesamte Abgas und die gesamte Ladeluft strömen über den linken Abgasturbolader, bis der gewünschte Ladedruck erreicht wird.

Turbinen- (4) und Verdichterzuschaltventil (3) sind geschlossen. Das Abgas der rechten Zylinderreihe strömt über das Querrohr (6) zur linken Turbine. Der rechte Abgasturbolader ist noch nicht in Betrieb. Das Bypassventil (2) ist geschlossen.

Geregelter Einladerbetrieb
Liegt der gewünschte Ladedruck an und ist mehr Abgasenergie vorhanden, als der Abgasturbolader für den Ladedruck benötigt, wird der Rest der Abgase über die rechte Turbine abgeblasen. Dabei wird der rechte Abgasturbolader beschleunigt.

Das Bypassventil (2) ist geschlossen und das Turbinenzuschaltventil (4) regelt den Ladedruck.

Durch das Hochlaufen des rechten Abgasturboladers beginnt der rechte Verdichter Luft zu fördern. Bei geschlossenem Vedichterzuschaltventil (3) strömt die Luft über ein Entlüftungsventil (8) vor den linken Verdichter und wird von diesem angesaugt.

Zuschaltung:
Können beide Abgasturbolader ab einer bestimmten Drehzahl ausreichend mit Abgasenergie versorgt werden, schaltet sich der rechte Abgasturbolader zu.

Mit dem vollständigen Öffnen des Turbinenzuschaltventils (4) und dem Schließen des Entlüftungsventils (8) wird die Zuschaltung eingeleitet. Der Druck hinter dem rechten Verdichter steigt stark an und öffnet das Verdichterzuschaltventil.

Zweite Stufe – oberer Drehzahlbereich Doppelladerbetrieb
Beide Abgasturbolader teilen sich die Ladeluft und die erforderliche Abgasenergie zu je 50%.
Die überschüssige Abgasenergie wird über ein Bypassventil abgeblasen.

Das Turbinenzuschaltventil (4) und das Verdichterzuschaltventil (3) sind ganz geöffnet. Das Entlüftungsventil (8) ist geschlossen. Die Regelung des Ladedrucks erfolgt über das Bypassventil (2). Der Ablauf ist microprozessor gesteuert.

Ladedruckaufbau Registeraufladung 959
Ladedruck
Drehzahl in 1/min
„Registeraufladung"
Konventionelle Doppelaufladung

ABOVE, 1987: *The engine features twin turbochargers of different capacities operating sequentially. This two-stage system, comprising a series of by-pass valves and crossover manifolds, completely eliminates turbo-lag and provides proportional boost pressures. Initially, one turbocharger operates alone providing boost from low revs. As the engine speed rises, so the second turbocharger is phased-in until at around 4000rpm both units are operating at full efficiency to send the engine singing towards the 7800rpm limit.*

INDEX

K

L

M

N

O

P